KEEP 'EM SINGING

JOY MACKENZIE & LYNN HODGES

ZondervanPublishingHouse
Grand Rapids, Michigan

A Division of HarperCollinsPublishers

Keep 'Em Singing
Copyright © 1993 by Joy MacKenzie

Requests for information should be addressed to:
Zondervan Publishing House
Grand Rapids, Michigan 49530

Library of Congress Cataloging-in-Publication Data

MacKenzie, Joy.
   Keep 'em singing : 101 simple and creative ideas for children's
music directors / Joy MacKenzie and Lynn Hodges.
     p. cm.
   Includes index.
   ISBN 0-310-48221-6 (paper)
   1. Choral singing—Juvenile—Instruction and study. 2. Church
work with children. 3. Children's choirs. I. Hodges, Lynn.
II. Title.
MT915.M22   1993
782.7'145—dc20   93-24634
                                                      CIP
                                                      MN

Edited by Tim McLaughlin
Illustrated by Gayle Seaberg Harvey
Interior design by Jack Rogers
Cover design by Larry Taylor Design

Printed in the United States of America

93 94 95 96 97 98 / ML / 10 9 8 7 6 5 4 3 2 1

To Nathan, whose growing intellectual curiosity
keeps his mom alive and alert.
To Libby, whose unbridled enthusiasm makes her mom's day.
To all the talented young people who have inspired our
musical efforts through the years.
We thank you!

TABLE OF CONTENTS

FOREWORD 9
HOW TO USE THIS BOOK 10

PRELUDE
What every kids' choir director should know. 13
    How to build a solid children's choir program 13
    In-class musical experiences for preschoolers through sixth graders 15
    Out-of-class musical experiences for preschoolers through sixth graders 15
    When rehearsals begin, your expectations must change 16
    Where to find good ideas and resources 17

The musical presentation 19
    Choose the right material. 19
    Before you start rehearsals... 20
    Now for rehearsals! 21
    Polish the performance—make it sparkle! 22

PRESTO! Easy, Ready-to-Use Classroom Activities
Staccato: Quick and easy five-minute fillers 27
    High-Low, Roof-Toe 27
    Vocal Volley 27
    Tongue Twisters 27
    Frisbee Frolic 28
    Fill-In Fun 28
    Bean Bag Boggler 28
    Pass the Hat 29
    Who Am I? 29
    Toes in a Row 29
    Kids Are Conduct-able! 30
    Lost in the Fog 30
    Soaring Melodies 30
    Sing a Sign! 30

Allegro: Short and fast activities (5-15 minutes) 31
    Getting to Know You (singing/ice-breaker) 31
    Bells on Their Toes (rhythm) 32
    Hole Notes (identifying lines and spaces, whole notes) 33
    Vertical or Horizontal? (hymn content) 34
    The Do-Re-Mi Mob (scales, note identification) 35
    Notable Answers (writing notes on a staff) 36
    Steppin' High (rhythm) 37
    Echo Box (listening skills/ear training) 38
    Everybody Jump! (naming notes) 39

Popcorn or Noodle?? (staccato, legato) 40
Add-On Art (music symbols) 41
Copy Cats ((rhythm mime) 43
Body Percussion (rhythm) 44
Tap Rap (rhythm guessing game) 45
Word Wizards (learning, reviewing song lyrics) 46
Joybells (rhythm instruments) 47
I'm Going to Join the Symphony (instruments of the orchestra) 48
Songs in Motion (memorizing songs and hymns) 49
In the Know (get-acquainted game/music or Bible review). 50
Finger Play (keyboard recognition). 51
Bones and Tones (warm up/chromatic scale/rhythm) 52
When the Music Stops (music symbols/general review—musical or biblical) 53
Standing Tall (sight reading) 54
Slow and Speedy (fast and slow tempo) 55
Pizza Party! (team game—reinforcement/review for any subject) 56
Ten Quick Questions (review any subject) 57
It's in the Bag (naming lines and spaces) 58
Major/Minor Quiz (distinguishing between major and minor chords). 59
Silly Symphony (following the conductor) 60
Diatonically Opposed (diatonic scale—a relay game) 61
Key Scan (keyboard/sharps and flats) 62
How Note-able R U? (naming notes) 63

Moderato: 20-45 minute activities 64
Back to the Drawing Board (memorizing songs or hymns). 64
Praise Rattles (rhythm/craft activity) 65
Toe-Re-Mi Chorus (singing for fun). 66
Hop a Whole Step, Half Step (identifying whole steps, half steps). 67
Musical Pantomime (independent drama activity) 68
Read Me a Story! (identifying and interpreting music dynamics, tempos) 69
Hymn-Knowledgy (identifying music symbols) 70
Finger Singers (diatonic scale). 71
Twist and Tangle (active music symbols game) 72
Hum a Number (singing the scale/Bible quiz) 74
Go Fishing! (music symbols) 75
There's Music in the Air (musical mobiles—craft project) 76
Search and Compose (composing a melody line) 78

Largo: Long-term activities and projects 79
Say It with Pictures (illustrating song lyrics) 79
Composers' Corner (writing/composing) 80
Meet and Greet (personalized introduction of group members) 81
Angel Cone Choir (craft project/singing for fun) 82
Glory All Around Us! (art project/illustrating a psalm) 84
Praise Graffiti (praise experience) 85

Water Music (ear training/pitch/melodic line/intervals/scales) 86
ABC Psalm (writing a psalm) 88
Sound Incorporated (listening/creating sound imitations) 89
Castle Choir (performance stage set for puppets and people) 90
Just My Size! (action songs and games/drama/movement) 91
Litany of Praise (composing an original litany) 92
Sock Singers (craft project/singing for fun) 94

MEDLEY A Variety of Extra-Special Activities for Children's Choir

Student activity sheets 97
Sol-Fa Songbird (sol-fa scale) 97
Mix and Match (music vocabulary/music symbols) 98
Up and Down the Mountain (sol-fa scale) 99
Old Testament Orchestra (ancient biblical instruments) 100
Add 'Em Up! (note values) 101
Jumbled Joy (sight reading/sequencing a melody) 102
Bible Instrument Rhymes 'n' Riddles (ancient biblical instruments/Scripture search) 103
Silly Scenario (music vocabulary) 105
World Music Series (sequencing music symbols and words) 107
Musical Munchies (naming notes) 108
The Eyes Have It! (music vocabulary word search) 109
Picture Puzzler (music symbols) 110
Music Madness (creative art with music symbols) 111
All about Me (getting to know one another) 112

Nine new songs 113
Rhythm! 113
Marching to a Steady Beat 113
Loud-Soft 114
Melody 114
The Music Family Alphabet 114
SATB Songs 115
So, Fa, Mi Song 115
We Are Children—Canon 115
Ancient Instruments of Praise 116

Quick reference song list 118
Action Songs 118
Praise Songs 118
Scripture Songs 118
Rounds, Canons, and Counter Melodies 118
Bible-Story Songs 118
Quiet Songs, Prayer-Time Songs 119
Hymns Kids Should Know 119
Play Songs 119

Six creative quiet times (devotionals) 120
    Sense-sational Creator! 120
    Psalm 100 121
    Worshiping Together 122
    Litany for Children's Choir 124
    Joy 125
    We Are the Body of Christ 126

Three short performance pieces 127
    Creation Rap 127
    An Easter Celebration 128
    Introit for Christmas 129

Kaleidoscope of ideas for kids' choirs 130

GRACE NOTES A Few Frills
Tool sheets 132
    Life-size Keyboard 132
    Labeled Keyboard, Diatonic Scale 133
    Grand Staff 134
    Short Staffs 135
    Open Staffs 136
    Flash Cards 137

Bulletin boards 141
    We Praise Him (positive reinforcement/praise) 141
    Setting Sail for a Sensational Choir Season (recruiting) 142
    Missing Person (recruiting) 143
    All by Yours-"Elf" Scale (key signatures) 144
    Great Is the Lord! (praise art) 145
    The Early Songbirds Get the Worms (attendance, punctuality) 146

A graded guide to musical knowledge 147
Conducting patterns 148
Basics in singing 149
Resources—publishers and titles of music and books 151

POSTLUDE Time Savers for Teachers
Clip art 156
A brief music glossary 168
Goofy glossary 174
Answer page 175

FOREWORD

Whether you are one who chose to work with a children's music program, or whether you were chosen—in *Keep 'Em Singing* you will find a wealth of how-to information, a collection of music-related games, puzzles, projects and crafts, rhythm activites, and songs for preschool through elementary age children. Here are dozens of practical and ready-to-do activities, timesaving devices, and lots of encouragement for motivating, managing, and leading children in meaningful musical experiences.

If you are a highly creative, multi-skilled musician with much positive experience with children's choirs, *Keep 'Em Singing* will provide you with professional reinforcement and a few fresh ideas. On the other hand, lesser skilled leaders or altogether nonmusicial adults who have been coerced into leadering a children's choir will find in this collection a wealth of life-saving resources.

Musically inclined or not, you will discover a cache of sparkling ideas that bring new fun, energy, spirit, and substance to your children's music program.

Keep 'Em Singing also contains sections about the administration, organization, discipline, and performances of a children's choir. And you'll find teacher helps and time savers in the form of bulletin boards, flash cards, parent-communication models, devotionals, clip art, resource lists, a simple music glossary, and short performance pieces.

The "Medley" section of *Keep 'Em Singing* contains a sparkling group of student activity pages designed for independent use by students. With the purchase of one copy of this book, permission is granted to reproduce these pages in the quantity needed for any one class or group of individuals. This permission also applies for "Nine New Songs" (page 113), "Three Short Performance Pieces" (page 127), "Tool Sheets" (page 132), "Bulletin Boards" (page 141), and "Clip Art" (page 156).

HOW TO USE THIS BOOK

We like to think of the pages of this book as confetti—a variety of fun, colorful, celebratory ideas for learning about music and making music with children.

When you toss confetti into the air, you never know exactly how or where it will land. So with this collection of ideas. The activities and experiences outlined in this book are not meant as formulas, but rather as tools and materials that give teachers and leaders a jumping-off place for many exciting and unpredictable landings. As you read the ideas, think how you can best use it or modify it to fit your situation. Choose and customize ideas in this book that will help you cultivate young singers and kindle their lively responses.

As musicians and educators, we find that the key to successful learning among children is vitality—precipitated by adult example. An enthusiastic Pied Piper can lead children almost anywhere. Undergird your enthusiam with careful preparation, however—preparation that, with *Keep 'Em Singing*, you can do with ease and with joy.

PRELUDE

PRELUDE

WHAT EVERY KID'S CHOIR DIRECTOR SHOULD KNOW

Not just any adult should work with children's music programs. It takes a special kind of woman or man. To be the director of a kids' choir (preschool to sixth grade), you need to still be part kid yourself. You've got to really believe that kids are the world's greatest resource and are far more capable and creative than most adults care to admit. You must possess the capacity for warm, healthy relationships with children and at least a moderate amount of musical knowledge and skill. A few organizational and management skills are necessary, especially when it comes to enlisting the support of some choice adults to assist you.

There's little if any prestige in directing a children's music program. It's physically and mentally exhausting. You will likely get a low budget, a disagreeable space, archaic equipment, and an impossible schedule. Job performance is subject to high criticism and low appreciation. So why work with a children's music program?

Here's why!

- You apparently know some notable facts not widely understood by the general population: that a human mind is quickest and sharpest at absorbing and retaining information between the ages of two and eight...that humans are most spiritually sensitive during this same stage in life...that among two-to-twelve-year-olds is more talent, energy, and focused interest per cubic inch than among any others.
- You can prepare kids for real life. You become the teacher and model of life-affecting spiritual concepts.
- Group participation and interaction toward common goals—especially public performances—help youngsters cultivate healthy self-concepts and social skills.
- From you, children can receive musical knowledge that provides life-long enjoyment for them in congregational singing, listening appreciation, and cultural awareness—not to mention the gift of a glorious tool for the praise and worship of their Creator.
- Working with kids keeps you young at heart, physically agile, and spiritually alive.
- Most kids are naturally motivated by music. It's part of their everyday life. The challenge is to use this interest for good, to the best advantage of their spiritual growth and awareness.

HOW TO BUILD A SOLID CHILDREN'S CHOIR PROGRAM

Whether your program is conducted daily, weekly, or seasonally, here's how you can lead a children's choir, without going *loco, poco a poco*. Execute these three aspects with energetic commitment!

PLAN!

Before each class meeting, take the time to think through the entire period of time you will spend with the children. Outline each experience, prepare the music, plan more activities than you can possibly use, and arrive early enough to arrange the physical setting for optimum use.

Every session should include a variety of short activities—the younger the children, the shorter the activities. This doesn't, of course, preclude long-term activities done in short pieces over a period of time. Remember to include brief three-to-six-minute breaks for talking, relaxing, and snacking.

Kids love special incentives, too...

- On-timers' prizes—all kids in their seats at six o'clock sharp get one.
- Achievement awards—as soon as individual kids have learned the song or script or Scripture, they get a special tape or book.
- Conduct reinforcement—the best worker takes the banner home for the week.
- Surprise treats—every once in a while, for no good reason!

Finally, allow sufficient time for your own mental and spiritual preparation. Take a deep breath...let it out slowly. Pray for energy, and pray for your students by name.

A note about discipline in a children's choir: Plan how you will deal with chronic talkers and pesterers—and the outright disobedient, disrespectful, and disruptive—before class begins. Better yet, you can prevent such problems as these by keeping things moving fast and by using positive reinforcement.

When the preventive approach doesn't work, and you *must* address negative behavior, we've found that talking and mild disruptions are best handled by isolating the offenders from the group. Persistent disobedience and disrespect, on the other hand, are almost always remedied by expulsion from the group (at least temporarily), followed by a parent conference.

DELEGATE!

Surround yourself with a team of competent, reliable helpers. First, get a bouncer. Recruit a big, friendly bruiser of a college student who enjoys kids.

Then create a cadre of "worker bees" responsible for keeping records, reserving rooms, scheduling, preparing materials, acting as music librarian, collecting equipment, communicating with parents, implementing a prayer chain, conducting sectional rehearsals, running errands, substituting for you, staffing learning centers, and supervising activity groups and teams. As you can see, some of these posts require a musical person, but most don't.

It's easier to recruit these helpers if you ask them to be responsible for *one specific task that they see as important*, but not overwhelming.

And don't think that adults must fill all these positions. Middle-grade kids make good team leaders and can reliably assist you with tasks such as attendance, the music library, phoning, advertising, the prayer chain, among others.

Some children's choir directors fortify their positions with a small advisory board or audition panel who are on call for decision making and general support.

Finally, you cannot give these helpers too many words and acts of appreciation.

COLLECT!

For the choir's success and your sanity, your best insurance policy is a stockpile of ready, accessible resource materials. You will draw on them for long-term and daily planning as well as for emergency, on-the-spot, fill-in activities. Some must-haves:

- **Resource books.** Look for ideas for games, activities, and recipes—and not necessarily music-related, either. Many general ideas are easily adapted to musical use. (Some good resource books are listed in the bibliography.)
- **Durable floor mats or posters.** They should bear often-used symbols (treble staff, grand staff, two-octave keyboard, for example).
- **Game mats.** Use them to teach musical symbols, lyrics, Scripture verses—virtually anything—whether in small groups or in big-time team competition (Twister, hopscotch, and tic-tac-toe are favorites).
- **Flash cards.** Great for teaching, reviewing, and reinforcing musical notes, symbols, dynamics, vocabulary, etc.
- **Tape recorder and tape library.** Don't get caught without a *working* cassette

player and an updated store of sing-along, story, and activity tapes for singing, marching, drawing, acting, etc. (see the bibliography). Always have several blank tapes that kids can use for recording their own creations.

- **Supply chest.** It's not easy to maintain a fresh and accessible supply of chalk, markers, construction paper, mural paper, masking tape, scissors, crayons, pencils, paste, staples, staplers, and pins. And beware of depending on left-over Sunday school supplies; sooner or later, you'll be caught short.
- **Keyboard and rhythm instruments.** Portable and homemade are okay!

A final note on collectibles such as these: If you have no music office, store these items in several labeled cardboard file boxes. Decorate them with musical symbols. Better yet, write DANGER—EXPLOSIVES on them to discourage borrowers and thieves.

IN-CLASS MUSICAL EXPERIENCES FOR PRESCHOOLERS THROUGH SIXTH GRADERS

Variety is crucial. Your audience, remember, is the "Sesame Street" generation.

A TYPICAL CLASS: KEEP IT VARIED!

Design a simple sequence of varied experiences for each class. For instance, a thirty-minute class for preschoolers and kindergartners could include a game, an action song, a quiet time with sentence prayers, a rhythm experience, then conclude with popcorn.

Though most of each class needs to be devoted to music or worship, include regular non-singing activities, too—art, dance, mime, rhythm, rap, choral reading, litany, games (both active and quiet), puppets, and construction projects. Why not create a puppet show with both singing and speaking, staged in a cardboard-box theater? (For more ideas

along these lines, see "A Kaleidoscope of Ideas" later in this book.)

PLAN A CLASS AROUND A SINGLE SONG.

Build a class experience on a single song—"Only a Boy Named David" or "The Wise Man and the Foolish Man," for example. Start the class by listening to the song played by an instrument or on a commercial tape. Then sing along, and add actions. Next tell or review the relevant Bible story with flannel board, drama, tape, or video. Finally, children can pretend to be photographers: As they listen to the song or story, they decide at what point they want to "photograph" the action—that is, translate onto paper via crayon, marker, or paint. You can spend the last few minutes of class sharing the "snapshots" and singing the song again.

Or try some variations of this single-song ideas. A pair or small group of children can prepare a written introduction and conclusion to the song that incorporate relevant Scriptures; other kids decide how to portray key characters or elements in the song (rain, floods, winds, soldiers, giants).

PLAN A CLASS AROUND A THEME.

Love, friends, animals, monsters, whole notes, major keys, minor keys, and musical dynamics all work well. Or base a class on an *idea*, such as *everything backwards*.

USE YOUR OLDER CHILDREN.

Assign them the planning of single, short events or activities to include in such class sessions—a mime or a vignette of a song, for example.

OUT-OF-CLASS MUSICAL EXPERIENCES FOR PRESCHOOLERS THROUGH SIXTH GRADERS

The high point of the year does not have to be a grand program or a huge musical—

particularly for the least motivated children in your choir, or for those least able to carry leading musical roles. For these kids variety is crucial. Here are two broad kinds of events in which *all* children can play important and satisfying parts.

SHORT-PERFORMANCE PROGRAMS.

Plan two to four a year, each with only three or four weeks of rehearsal. They offer better distribution of roles and responsibilities than one big annual performance.

OUTREACH AND SERVICE.

Define opportunities in which children have a dignified part in leading a worship service, visiting a hospital or retirement home, or assuming responsibility for the opening assembly of an adult Sunday school class. Or take a short, sparkling singing-speaking puppet show on the road, perhaps to a nearby inner city or border city.

WHEN REHEARSALS BEGIN, YOUR EXPECTATIONS MUST CHANGE

The enjoyable process of learning and working together is different from rehearsing for a performance. Inherent in performing is the obligation to perform to the best of one's ability. Yes, children's choirs in churches and schools perform at least partially and usually primarily for the benefit of the children, not of the audience. Yet the performance experience requires that children give their best and most exacting work for their audience. After all, an audience deserves a performance that is both understandable and enjoyable.

So young performers need to know from the first day of rehearsal that *expectations will be high and serious*. Performance expectations for a single, simple song at a worship service are the same as for the staging of a major musical. Let them know that during the preparation for any performance, they will be treated as young professionals.

To meet such a level of expectation, engage children in an agreement or contract:

* Performers will be faithful to all rehearsals. (They will call if they must be absent.)
* Performers will be on time to all rehearsals—and that means seated and ready to work.
* Performers will be extremely *attentive* and *hard-working* during each rehearsal.
* The director will be on time and have the physical setting and music ready.
* The director will make work fast, fun, and interesting.
* The director will plan short breaks for talking and relaxing—with treats sometimes, too!
* The director will stick to the schedule so performers and parents can make exact plans.

An agreement like this is taken more seriously if it is written, signed by both performer and director, and a copy sent home. (This practice informs parents as well as students of your expectations.) Children and parents have always welcomed this procedure whenever we've used it. It ensures a secure, easy, productive working relationship. After only one rehearsal, kids recognize the difference between *rehearsal* expectations and the more relaxed and less disciplined climate of non-rehearsal classes. And believe us, they really like high, serious expectations!

A FEW NOTES ABOUT REHEARSALS...

* When preparing for any performance, large or small, emphasize and review often the purpose for performance: *To communicate the message and to minister.* Performances are not merely to entertain, impress, or perform for one's own satisfaction.
* Give attention to details other than singing and staging. How a group walks to and from the performance area, for

instance, may be as important as what they sing and say. Don't just *talk* about these details—*practice* them!

- Videotape performances and ask kids to later critique them.
- Perform often!

WHERE TO FIND GOOD IDEAS AND RESOURCES

- **Scour children's activity, idea, and make-and-do books.** A wide variety are available in school-supply stores, Christian book stores, children's libraries, and even in general bookstores. When you find a good general idea, adapt it for use as a music and worship activity.

- **Visit toy stores.** It's amazing how many wild and crazy ideas pop into one's mind when lost in a maze of child's play materials. Tinker, putter, dream, and let your mind run free.

- **Keep your eyes open for creative displays in grocery and department stores.** They often trigger great ideas— and occasionally stores discard used displays and let you have them for the asking.

- **Watch kids' TV shows—the good ones, that is.** Beware of evil icons, characters who claim supernatural powers, and programs with a cultic or New Age orientation. On the other hand, note the motivation, the strategy, the pacing in kids' shows. Remember that Old Testament and New Testament miracles far out-thrill Disney and Ripley.

- **Preschool and elementary school classrooms are a great hunting ground.** Talk to creative teachers. Beg, borrow, and modify their suggestions.

- **Your plain old book and music stores is where you can get music in all forms.** It is also available from individual publishers and distributors. (A list of publishing houses and distribution centers that handle Christian product for children is found beginning on page 151.)

THE MUSICAL PRESENTATION

A MASTER PLAN OF ACTION FOR CHOOSING, PREPARING, PRODUCING, POLISHING, AND PERFORMING

CHOOSE THE RIGHT MATERIAL.

CONTENT

Only occasionally do children deal consciously with spiritual values and ideas. Using this time wisely means choosing performance pieces whose content has life-changing value. Will it be fluff or food for thought?

A fine point worth remembering as you choose music: If the music carries doctrinal views, do they agree with those of your church? (If they don't, you can easily alter dialogue and narration to fit your situation.)

How will the audience be affected by the message? And will the adults on the production end of things (staff, parents, and so on) feel the project is worthy of their time and effort—training, contributing props, costumes, food, transportation?

MUSIC

Will the children enjoy the material? Are the songs fun? At least eighty percent of the program should be fun, cute, cool—whatever the "in" sound and style is for today's kids. And is there enough variety in style and tempo to make the work interesting? Are the ranges comfortable for your children's voices?

Do the length of the work and the level of difficulty suit your group? Don't hesitate to edit the music—create more or fewer solos, let a child speak a solo, borrow assistance from an outside source (such as an older age group), split a solo, etc.

ADAPTABILITY

Can the work be effectively presented in your physical setting? Can it be rehearsed and prepared within your time frame? Can all children have satisfying roles? Try to assign each child an identification that he or she sees as important—in other words, something more than "Choir" or "Boy 3."

Can the songs and material be used appropriately in other settings? Will parts of the presentation translate into contexts such as a morning worship service, a Children's Day event, a nursing home or chapel service, or collaborative use with youth or adult choirs?

PRACTICALITY AND ECONOMICS

Can the sets, props, and costumes be managed in your setting? Can they be transported easily if the presentation travels?

Is the production feasible within your budget? (Don't forget that much can be done on a beg, borrow, and barter basis. So don't be afraid to ask for donations. Just give credit in the program!) If you can't get what the script prescribes, come up with an outrageous substitute. In fact, use the opportunity to start or add to a costume and props collection. (Summer is a great time to work on building and refurbishing such a collection.)

Is the production worth the hassle? Can it be executed so that your staff and helpers will want to be involved in future performances? Count the cost ahead of time!

How much value can you get out of the

material for future use? Can you use a song as an anthem at a later date, for instance? Are you likely to reuse props and costumes?

BEFORE YOU START REHEARSALS...

RECRUIT A STAFF. YOU PROBABLY CAN'T LIVE WITHOUT THESE PEOPLE, SO ENLIST THEM EARLY:

- *Producer.* A self-starter, dependable, accountable, likeable—a communicator, at least. The producer needs to be part magician, not necessarily a musician. Enlist a producer you won't have to baby constantly...a liaison between the director and the production crew...the choir's "banker" and budget keeper...informer, motivator, and applauder for all crew, cast, and assistants...the one who orders music, tapes, and equipment...who makes arrangements for use of space and of equipment...who gets a task done for the director.
- *Music assistant.* Capable of conducting extra rehearsals...present at most rehearsals...assists as needed.
- *Costume coordinator.* Calls moms, buys material, executes sewing needs, and arranges back-stage space for costume storage and changing.
- *Props manager.* Creates, gathers, and returns props—and may assist stage manager.
- *Stage manager.* Coordinates sets, props, sound, and lights to create the stage setting. (Kids can be part of a stage crew to assist during rehearsals as well as performances.)
- *Communications chairman.* Works with you (the director) and the producer to create printed programs and communications with parents and staff. Also in charge of advertising and publicity—bulletin announcements, posters, fliers, signs, contacting the media and other churches, etc.

- *Refreshments coordinator.* For rehearsals and performances.
- *Transportation coordinator.* Should the show hit the road!
- *Light technician.*
- *Sound technician.*
- *Make-up person.*

Give each of these people a specific job description, complete with schedule, deadlines, budget restrictions, and whatever special instructions they need. You have a ministry to the people who assist you. Recognize the efficient execution of their jobs with obvious appreciation and support—and encourage the rest of the team to thank them, too. Everyone needs to feel important because they *are* important.

Schedule everything. Create your calendar—every aspect of it: auditions, rehearsals, performances, including times and places. Because the dates you write down affect more than *your* schedule, coordinate them with other important activities that involve your kids, staff, and parents. Based on your calendar, now prepare schedules and to-do lists for the production staff.

Determine your expectations for the cast—now, before any auditions. What are your requirements for auditions? What behavior and decorum will you insist on during rehearsals? What are your procedures for absence and tardiness? Write these in letter form, then mail them to prospective cast members.

Decide how you will conduct auditions. It's a good idea to get some help here—two or more advisors, for instance, who understand the goals and purposes of the performance experience and who can help you assign parts.

Plan your first rehearsal now—*before* it arrives. In fact, decide how you will handle every moment in it. Make the first rehearsal a joyful, meaningful, hardworking experience for both cast and staff. (Everyone there needs to know that any performance done well requires much hard work.)

Communicate your plans to children and their parents. To all prospective cast members, mail an invitation either to audition or to join the performance group. Use enrollment lists from Sunday school or day school, advertise on a poster, announce in public meetings—whatever gets the word out. If necessary, promise everyone a speaking part!

After auditions, send written communication to both children and parents regarding the schedule, your expectations about attendance and behavior, and as much early information about costumes, performances, etc., as is available. Ask parents for any assistance you need. Give parents a phone number (preferably not yours) to call for attendance, questions, and emergencies.

Now for rehearsals!

The first rehearsal

Present the entire schedule for performance preparation...Review expectations for cast members (including attendance and behavior), and distribute the contract (see page 16)...Very briefly, introduce the musical—the big message, your purpose for doing it, the characters, setting, etc.

Right away, learn the *most exciting* song, and choreograph at least part of it.

Now, just before the first rehearsal ends, give each child three items:

- A copy of the musical score, so they can see what's ahead and get a feel for the big picture.
- A cassette tape of particular songs, scripts, or of the entire musical or show. Discuss its use in learning and memorizing songs and script. (If you cannot afford a commercial tape for each child, ask parents to purchase tapes—or contact the show's publisher for permission to make amateur rehearsal tape copies that you promise to destroy after the show.)
- A deadline for knowing the first song or

two. (See appendix for more information.) And just for fun, think about kicking off your first rehearsal with a theme party!

Subsequent rehearsals

Plan each rehearsal to include many short, fast-moving sections. Arrive at the rehearsal space ahead of time in order to have the room and music ready. When rehearsal begins, intersperse hard work with fun breaks for snacks, relaxation, restroom, and casual conversation. When you're working, on the other hand, require absolute attention and accountability.

Two key words: *variety* and *pacing*. So plan several short work sections: Begin by learning new material...then work briefly on choreography for the same sections...move on to refining the children's diction or phrasing. In other words, mix easy and difficult; mix fast and slow tempos; mix unison and harmony sections.

If you have a musical assistant or two, occasionally conduct two or three rehearsals at the same time. Use your assistant to work with solos or drama, for example, while you focus on harmony or choreography.

Take time to discuss any biblical lessons that are in the musical. Spend some brief time praying about specific needs of the group members, as well as for God's blessing and direction in the preparation and performance of the musical, that the message will be heard and understood.

Stick to the schedule so parents can count on times and dates. Finally, be a cheerleader, disciplinarian, educator, friend, and spiritual reinforcer!

Two notes on staging and blocking

- Create a tentative plan for the *complete* staging and blocking *on paper* before you try to implement it—but don't be afraid to change it a dozen times after you've seen real bodies in the real space.
- Before you put the entire cast on stage,

block and rehearse the major roles first.

POLISH THE PERFORMANCE—MAKE IT SPARKLE!

FACIAL EXPRESSION

Eyes wide, eyebrows up...Face alive and alert—let your *face* tell the story!...Show your teeth—*smile!*...Lean forward slightly to create energy, urgency...Scan the audience with your eyes.

CHOREOGRAPHY

It must be crisp and snappy...Every move should be deliberate and on purpose...Keep it simple and easy to remember...Plan most of the choreography from the waist up, with little or no footwork—feet can rarely be seen past the third row, anyway...Place uncoordinated kids in back, or block them separately...Allow kids to be involved in planning at least some of the choreography—they have great ideas.

DRAMA

Children should vary their vocal inflection—loud to stage whisper, dramatic pauses, emotion...They must use their hands, and keep their elbows away from their waists...Project! Speak to the back row!...Always face to the audience!...Never stand with back to audience!...Never stand directly in front of or behind anyone else!...All actors on stage should focus their attention on where the action or conversation is...Articulate! Speak more slowly than is comfortable...Never speak over laughs or applause, but wait to speak until it's *almost* over...Communicate! Talk to the people—it's not their job to listen, but your job to make them hear and understand...Achieve energy by adding intensity to voice and body movement.

MUSIC

Let the music be simple if you want, but if you expect an audience to listen, the music must be well done...Make it *clean, clear* and *exact*— enunciate, pronounce correctly, make entrances and cut-offs clean...Whether the tempo is fast or slow, the volume loud or soft, children must project excitement, urgency, energy...Actors should freeze after a song, then have one person lead the "break" during silence or applause...Make use of "canned" voices on split tracks to fill out choir sound.

TECHNICAL STUFF

If you want a successful performance, the people you need most are your light and sound crew. Love them! Miking moving kids is a sound technician's nightmare. Be patient and supportive, yet insist on technical excellence and rehearsal time. *The entire purpose of a performance is lost if it cannot be heard and seen!*

- Mark books for light and sound people, as well as for any other assistants who need to know *where* in the script something happens.
- Have the first technical rehearsal alone with the sound and light crew.
- Be sure the technical crew is present and prepared for the children's dress rehearsal.
- Invite a friendly outside critic to one or more of the last rehearsals to take notes and point out things you haven't noticed.
- Make arrangements for clean-up and return of borrowed equipment after the last performance.
- Make arrangements for someone to video tape the performance so the kids can watch themselves, perhaps at the cast party.

ABOUT CONDUCTING

Mirror the choreography for kids. Remember that during performances your cues must be done where the audience can't see you. Wearing black helps.

- Keep their expressions alive by exuding excitement in your own face and body.
- Conducting every beat is *not* necessary.

Simply keep them on track with a steady, recognizable beat.

- Cuing important entrances and choreography is crucial.

PRESTO

EASY, READY-TO-USE CLASSROOM ACTIVITIES

QUICK AND EASY FIVE-MINUTE FILLERS

HIGH-LOW, ROOF-TOE

Ask children to stand. Explain that when they hear you sing or play a high note, they are to reach up to the roof; when you sing or play a low note, they are to touch their toes. Repeat as time allows. Children can take turns being the leader, too.

VOCAL VOLLEY

Start a group sing-along song—one that you wish to review or a just-for-fun one. As you begin the song, toss a beach ball or large balloon into the air. Ask children to try to keep the balloon in the air as long as the song lasts, but allow it to touch the floor at the very moment the last note of the song is sung. And everyone must sing!

TONGUE TWISTERS

For five minutes of comical contortions, see how quickly your choir members can repeat these terrible tongue twisters:

Sixty songs sung sforzando
Decrescendo, diminuendo
Five fine fat fermatas
The baritone beat the bass to the bar line.
Glissando grandioso
Triple treble triplet
Staccato-ostinato-rubato
Hark! I hear a hawk humming a holy harmony!

Sixty songs sung....

FRISBEE FROLIC

Ask a review question about any musical or biblical subject, then toss a Frisbee. The child who catches it gets to answer the question. If he can't, he *hands* the frisbee to another classmate who thinks she has the answer. Only the one who answers your question correctly may *toss* it back to you. Then ask another question. See how many questions you can fit into five minutes!

FILL-IN FUN

Use the five minutes at the beginning or end of class or during a transition time to review Scripture or song lyrics. Simply begin quoting the words, but pausing before key words or phrases and pointing to various children to "fill in" those pauses with the appropriate words:

"Make a joyful noise unto the _____, all ye_____. Serve the Lord with _____. Come before his _____ with _____."

Repetition like this is highly motivating and fun for the kids. Pretty soon the words you review consistently in this manner will become a permanent part of their "repertoire."

BEAN BAG BOGGLER

Call out a word associated with music (the name of a note, symbol, musical form, style, a composer, a word denoting tempo, dynamics, etc.). As you call the word, toss a bean bag to a child. The child calls out a different "music word" and tosses the bag to a third child. Proceed until no one can think of a word.

Variation: This may be done with lyrics, books of the Bible, names of the choir members, and so on.

PASS THE HAT

This game is like musical chairs. Children stand in a line or circle. Place a hat or cap on one child's head. Play or sing a tune. When the music starts, the child takes the hat from his head and puts it on the head of the next child. Children continue passing the hat from one head to another in this fashion. The child who is wearing the hat when the music stops must sit down. Continue the game until only one child is left standing. Then all sing, "Hi-ho the derry-o, the hat stands alone!"

WHO AM I?

Ask children to watch closely as you pantomime playing an instrument—any instrument. When they think they can identify the specific instrument or family of instruments, they must raise their hand. Call on someone for the name of the instrument(s). Remember that several instruments appear to pantomime alike—the violin and viola, for instance. In that case, accept either answer.

Variations: Older children may write answers, or the exercise may be used as a team game.

TOES IN A ROW

To review lyrics or a Scripture memory verse—or as a creative way of making an important announcement—try this at the beginning or end of a class session.

As children arrive, write a word or two from the lyrics or verse on the bottom of each

child's bare feet (or on their palms). When you've used all the words, tell the children that they must arrange themselves in word order, sitting in a circle, bare feet facing in towards the center. Sing or say the entire message together.

KIDS ARE CONDUCT-ABLE!

Use brief left-over periods of time to practice conducting patterns with your young musicians. (Be sure to face the same direction that they are.) Choose a familiar tune. Hum it together and "conduct" it, using the proper pattern. (See "Conducting Patterns" on page XX.)

Variation: Conduct recorded music, too!

LOST IN THE FOG

Blindfold two pairs of children. The other children form a large, protective circle around the players—they are the "fog," within which one of each blindfolded pair is the "lost child," and their partner searches for them in the "fog."

Each pair has a different note. One searcher sings the syllable *la*, for example, and the other *mi*. The "lost" children listen carefully for their partner's note and try to match it. As the four intermittently sing out the notes back and forth to each other, they try to determine the location of their partners and get together. When the partners have found each other, they may give their blindfolds to new pairs.

SOARING MELODIES

Children pretend that one of their hands is an airplane. As you sing or play a melody or song, ask the children to "fly" their airplanes, making them go *up* if the melody goes up, *down* if the melody goes down. Of course, the airplane *glides* when the pitches of the melody stay about the same.

SING A SIGN!

Try this short, catchy method of reviewing music signs, symbols, and vocabulary (to the tune of "Are You Sleeping?").

I am thinking, I am thinking
Of a sign, of a sign.
If you choose to use it,
It will make the music
Oh so fine, oh so fine!

The child who is "It" thinks of a musical word, sign, symbol or dynamic. He sings the tune above, then writes his sign or word on the chalk board. Those who think they can tell the meaning of the word or symbol raise their hands, and "It" chooses someone. Whoever answers correctly becomes "It."

SHORT AND FAST ACTIVITIES
(5-15 MINUTES)

GETTING TO KNOW YOU
(SINGING/ICE-BREAKER)

TIME: 5-10 minutes

MATERIALS NEEDED: none

INSTRUCTIONS:

1. Ask the children to listen as you sing a melody (choose your own). Use the following words:

    "My name is _____. What is your name?"
    As you sing the melody, point to one child.

2. The child to whom you pointed answers, singing the same tune. She sings:

    "My name is _____. What is your name?"
    —and she points to another child.

3. The game continues until all children have been chosen and have sung their responses.

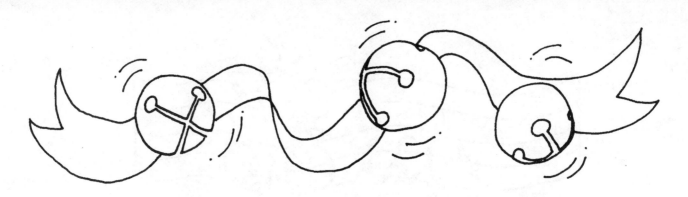

BELLS ON THEIR TOES
(RHYTHM)

TIME: 5-10 minutes

MATERIALS NEEDED:
- jingle bells (2-4 per child)
- yarn or ribbon

INSTRUCTIONS:

1. Attach jingle bells to children's shoes or to their bare toes.

2. Sing or play songs during which children use the bells as rhythm instrument accompaniment as they walk, march, or tap their feet.

VARIATION: During the Christmas season, do this at the end of a class session as a 5-10-minute filler. Then release children to parents with a merry jingle! Such a gift!

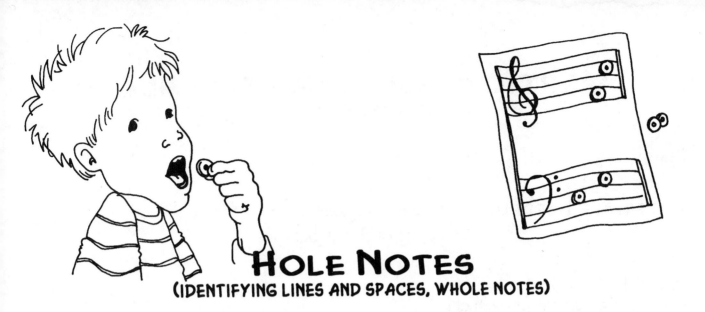

HOLE NOTES
(IDENTIFYING LINES AND SPACES, WHOLE NOTES)

TIME: 5-10 minutes

MATERIALS NEEDED:
- enlarged music staff (see page 134)
- candy Lifesavers (6 per child)

INSTRUCTIONS:

1. To each child give one piece of staff paper and *six* Lifesavers.

2. Discuss the characteristics of whole notes and point out that a Lifesaver looks very much like a whole note—just for fun, call it a "hole" note.

3. List on the chalkboard a group of *six* lines or spaces to be identified. Examples:
   - Treble clef, line F
   - Bass clef, space C
   - Treble clef, space E
   - Treble clef, line G
   - Bass clef, line A
   - Treble clef, space D

4. Ask children to locate each line or space listed by placing a "hole" note (a Lifesaver) in the correct position on their staff.

5. When all children have successfully completed the task, each may eat *one* Lifesaver.

6. Now present a new group of *five* lines and spaces to be identified, and repeat steps 3 and 4 above.

7. Continue in the same manner with four, three, two, and finally one line or space to be identified—and *all* Lifesavers are eaten! YUM!

VERTICAL OR HORIZONTAL?
(HYMN CONTENT)

TIME: 10 minutes

MATERIALS NEEDED:
- 1 hymnal for each child
- copies of church bulletins

INSTRUCTIONS:

1. Provide a hymnal for each child.

2. Call out the name and page number of a hymn.

3. Ask children to locate the hymn, scan the lyrics, and decide whether the message of the hymn is addressed to God (*vertical*) or directed to others *about* God or the Christian faith (*horizontal*).

4. Obtain copies of church bulletins from recent Sundays or for the coming Sunday, and review the meaning of each hymn listed. Decide how each is directed: Is it vertical or horizontal in its intent?

↑ VERTICAL.

← HORIZONTAL.

The Do-Re-Mi Mob
(Scales, Note Identification)

Time: 10-20 minutes

Materials Needed: • at least 8 human bodies

Instructions:

1. Ask eight children to stand in a row, facing the class.

2. Explain to all that this row of eight children represents a C major scale.

3. Ask the children representing the scale to speak their note names, starting with the C on the left.

4. Now instruct the class to observe as you "play" each note by touching the person representing that note on the head. Ask the class to sing each note name as you touch it. Touch the notes of the scale in sequence, moving up and down the scale several times.

5. Then ask students to sing note names as you point to them *out of sequence.*

6. When all children understand the scale concept, ask them if they recognize the familiar tune they are "singing." Use familiar, easy-to-recognize tunes. Examples:
   • Are You Sleeping? (1-2-3-1-1-2-3-1-3-4-5-3-4-5)
   • Joy To The World (8-7-6-5-4-3-2-1)
   • Three Blind Mice (3-2-1-3-2-1-5-4-4-3-5-4-4-3)
   • Joyful, Joyful (3-3-4-5-5-4-3-2-1-1-2-3-3-2-2)
   • Silent Night (5-6-5-3-5-6-5-3)

Variation:
   • Add human chromatics: Name sharps going up and flats going down.
   • The same activity may be done with a live keyboard—kids wearing black and white shirts, lying in the key positions.

NOTABLE ANSWERS
(WRITING NOTES ON A STAFF)

TIME: 10 minutes

MATERIALS NEEDED: • the "Short Staffs" sheet (see page 135)
• pencils

INSTRUCTIONS:

1. Provide for each child a copy of the "Short Staffs" sheet on which to record answers to the following statements. Answers are written not with words, but with notes on the staff.

   • Joseph found a silver cup in Benjamin's <u>B</u> <u>A</u> <u>G</u>.

   • Mary and Martha cried because Lazarus was __ __ __ __.

   • The lame man took up his __ __ __ and walked.

   • Jesus __ __ __ 5,000 people with a boy's lunch.

   • Jesus taught in the temple when he was 12 years of __ __ __.

   • When Stephen was stoned, his __ __ __ __ looked like that of an angel.

   • When you want a sum, you __ __ __.

   • The devil is __ __ __.

   • The Bible says you are to honor your mom and __ __ __.

2. Encourage children to use the remaining staffs to create additional words of their own and try them out in quiz form on their friends.

STEPPIN' HIGH
(RHYTHM)

TIME: 8-10 minutes

MATERIALS NEEDED: • any percussion instrument or reasonable facsimile

INSTRUCTIONS:

1. Ask one child to walk across the room and back to her seat. As she does so, mimic the rhythm of her footsteps with a percussive beat.

2. Repeat the process with several children.

3. Now ask the children to listen to you as you demonstrate a *steady* beat. They might identify which children (if any) have walked with a steady beat.

4. Ask a child who thinks he understands the meaning of *steady* to walk, stepping to the beat of the instrument.

5. Repeat with several children, varying the tempo slightly with each child.

6. Now try it in groups of three or four. As each group tries to step to the beat, other children may tap their hands on their knees.

ECHO BOX
(LISTENING SKILLS/EAR TRAINING)

TIME: 10 minutes

MATERIALS NEEDED:
- a cardboard box (or similarly suitable container), decorated with a musical theme

INSTRUCTIONS:

1. Say to the children, "I wonder if my Echo Box is working. If it is, you will repeat everything I say or do when I am in the box. If I sing, you will sing. If I clap a rhythm , you will clap the same rhythm. [*Whisper*] If I whisper, you will whisper back to me. Everyone must be *very* quiet in order for my Echo Box to work."

2. Slowly and dramatically step into the box.

3. Sing or clap simple, short tunes and rhythms. Children should echo exactly what you do.

4. The Echo Box is most intriguing and effective if used *only* for exactly what you want repeated by the children. If additional explanation or instruction is needed, step out of the box to do so.

VARIATION:

- Learn short passages of Scripture or hymns using the Echo Box.
- Allow children to take turns being inside the box.
- The Echo Box is a device that can become a long-term teaching tool. After just a few sessions, even very young children will know exactly how to respond. Use sparingly so that it will not lose its appeal.

EVERYBODY JUMP!
(NAMING NOTES)

TIME: 10-15 minutes

MATERIALS NEEDED: • 1 or more long jump ropes

INSTRUCTIONS:

1. Use two children to swing each rope. (Preschoolers may jump a swaying rope rather than one that is being turned.)

2. Assign no more than five players to each rope.

3. Give each player a note name: A B C D E, or F G A B C (optional: use the chromatic scale).

4. All players begin jumping together as they chant this rhyme:
   Sing to the Lord
   A brand new song
   Makin' music
   All day long!
   A (beat) B (beat) C (beat) D (beat) E, etc.

5. As each note name is called out in the final line of the rhyme, the child to whom that note is assigned jumps "out."

6. Now reverse the game: Repeat the chant as children jump *in* when they hear their note name.

VARIATION:

• Use the rhyme to teach any scale.
• Use the same idea to teach the books of the Bible, rhythms, etc.

POPCORN OR NOODLE?
(STACCATO, LEGATO)

TIME: 5-8 minutes

MATERIALS NEEDED: none

INSTRUCTIONS:

1. Children join you in forming a large circle.

2. Ask them to listen carefully as you say two very important words. They should try to identify the difference between how the two words (staccato and legato) are presented.

3. Say *sta' ca' to'* using short, abrupt, accented syllables. Then say *lehgahhto* using long, smooth syllables.

4. Discuss the meaning of each word and ask children to mimic the words as you say them several times.

5. Then say, "The word *staccato* reminds me of popping popcorn. When I say *staccato*, use your bodies to show me popcorn by jumping up and down like a piece of corn popping." Practice doing this!

6. Now say, "The word *legato* reminds me of a long, wet, wavy noodle. Let's join hands in a circle and make a long noodle. We can make it curly like this!" as the teacher raises her left arm, consequently raising the right arm of the child to her left. That child then raises his left arm and the "wave" continues around the circle until it returns to the teacher. "Isn't that fun? When I say *legato*, we'll do our 'noodle act!'"

7. Ask children to use these two body actions to identify first the spoken words as you call them out, then staccato or legato phrases played by an instrument.

VARIATION:

- Allow children to take turns being the leader. They may think of other musical terms that can be demonstrated with body language by the group.

Add-On Art
(Musical Symbols)

Time: 5-15 minutes

Materials Needed:
- pencils, crayons
- a copy of the "Add-On Art" activity sheet (see page 42)

Instructions:
1. Provide to each child one copy of the "Add-On Art" activity sheet, and give the following instructions, either orally or in writing:
   - Finish the bear by adding two whole notes (nose and tail).
   - Finish the stick man by adding one quarter note (leg and foot) and one F clef sign (ear).
   - Finish the bird by adding one crescendo sign (beak) and one decrescendo sign (wing).
   - Finish the crocodile by adding two fermatas (eyes).
   - Finish the magician's trick by adding a whole rest (hat).
   - Patch the pants by adding a sharp sign (patch).

2. Provide time and space for sharing and discussing finished product.

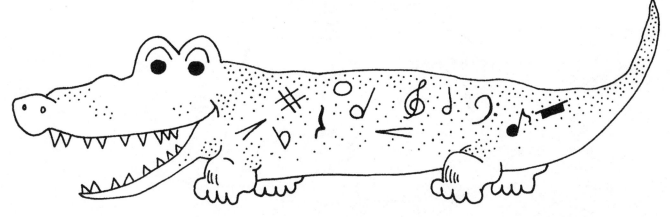

41

COPY CATS
(RHYTHM MIME)

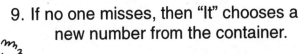

TIME: 10 minutes

MATERIALS NEEDED:
- masking tape
- felt marker
- numbered paper strips in a container

INSTRUCTIONS:

1. Seat children in a circle.

2. Number children by writing a numeral on masking tape and sticking it to each child's clothing.

3. Place in the center of the circle a container with paper strips bearing numbers corresponding to those worn by the children.

4. Ask a child to choose a number from the container. The child wearing the chosen number becomes "It."

5. "It" claps a rhythm to the classmate seated to his right in the circle.

6. The classmate tries to repeat the rhythm pattern.

7. If she is successful, "It" moves on to the next player and the next, and so on, until someone misses.

8. The one who misses chooses a new number from the container, and the person wearing that number becomes "It."

9. If no one misses, then "It" chooses a new number from the container.

10. Continue until all children have had turns.

VARIATION:
- With very young children, the teacher may always be "It."

43

BODY PERCUSSION
(RHYTHM)

TIME: 5-10 minutes

MATERIALS NEEDED: none

INSTRUCTIONS:

1. Demonstrate the wide variety of percussive effects provided by the human body—stomp, clap, click, cluck, hop, tap, smack, slap, knock, snap, sniff, etc.

2. Ask children to echo you as you create rhythm patterns using combinations of several "body percussion instruments."

3. Keep rhythms slow and steady.

4. Allow children to take turns leading.

VARIATION:

- May be used with the Echo Box (see page 38).

Tap Rap
(RHYTHM GUESSING GAME)

TIME: 10-15 minutes

MATERIALS NEEDED: none

INSTRUCTIONS:

1. Divide group into two teams.

2. The first player on team A taps on the back of the first player on team B the rhythm of a familiar song's first line.

3. If B can guess the song, B gets a point. If not, A gets the point.

4. Now switch—a team B player taps a rhythm on a team A player.

5. Play until all team members have had a turn or as long as time permits. The team with the most points wins.

VARIATION:

- The game may be more controlled if you provide song titles to be drawn from a hat.

WORD WIZARDS
(LEARNING, REVIEWING SONG LYRICS)

TIME: 10 minutes

MATERIALS NEEDED: • any object that is soft and safe to toss.

INSTRUCTIONS:

This is a hot-potato game. Any safe object may be used as the potato.

1. Seat children in a circle and give the "potato" to the first "Wizard."

2. Call out the name of a song whose lyrics you wish to review.

3. The Wizard passes the potato to his left as he begins reciting the song lyrics; he continues reciting as the potato is passed quickly from child to child around the circle.

4. When the potato returns to the Wizard, he stops reciting, tosses the object to someone else in the circle, and the new Wizard must continue the lyrics from where the first Wizard stopped.

5. Continue to the end of the song, or call out a new song title.

6. All players must listen carefully to make sure the Wizards recall the correct lyrics.

VARIATION:

• Use this game to review Bible verses or books of the Bible.

JOYBELLS
(RHYTHM INSTRUMENTS)

TIME: 15 minutes

MATERIALS NEEDED:
- an old-fashioned clothespin for each child
- large jingle bells (two per child)
- two 8-inch lengths of yarn per child
- scissors, glue, and felt-tip pen

INSTRUCTIONS:

1. Give each child one clothespin, two bells, two lengths of yarn, glue, and scissors.

2. Direct children to construct joybells:
   - String each bell on a piece of yarn.
   - Center the bell on the yarn and tie a knot.
   - Now tie the first bell tightly to the head of the clothespin. Make a knot and clip off the extra yarn. Put a drop of glue on the knot to secure it.
   - Do the same with the second bell, placing it on the opposite side of the clothespin head.
   - Use the marker to write on the clothespin: "Brianne's Joybell" (or any inscription you want).

I'm Going to Join the Symphony
(INSTRUMENTS OF THE ORCHESTRA)

TIME: 10-15 minutes

MATERIALS NEEDED: none

INSTRUCTIONS:

1. Seat children in a circle.

2. The first player says, "I'm going to join the symphony; I'll play the ———!" then mimics playing the instrument he chooses.

3. The second player says, "I'm going to join the symphony; I'll play the ——— [the first player's instrument, miming as she names it] and the ——— [her own instrument, and a mime]!"

4. The third player repeats players one and two, adding yet another instrument.

5. The game proceeds as long as time and interest allow.

VARIATION:

- Do this game to a rhythmic accompaniment of clapping or snapping.

Songs in Motion
(Memorizing Songs and Hymns)

TIME: 10-12 minutes

MATERIALS NEEDED: none

INSTRUCTIONS:
1. Get acquainted with this method of memorizing songs by practicing with a simple, familiar song or chorus. Sing it once or twice without motions.

2. Now replace one word with a motion. In "Jesus Loves Me," for example, instead of singing the word "Jesus," point to heaven.

3. Repeat the song, each time replacing an additional word with a motion.
4. Once you've replaced as many words as you wish, reverse the process: replace motions with words, until the song is sung as a whole without motions. By the time you complete this process, everyone will probably know the song's lyrics.

VARIATION:
- Learn Scripture verses this way, too.

In the Know
(Get-Acquainted Game/Musical or Bible Review)

Time: 5-10 minutes

Materials Needed: none

Instructions:

1. Seat children in a circle.

2. "It" stands in the center of the circle, closes his eyes, and turns around several times—then opens his eyes and directly faces one person in the circle.

   - If "It" folds his arms *in front* of his body, the person he faces must name a *girl* in the circle.

   - If "It" folds his arms *behind* his body, the person must name a *boy* in the circle.

   - The boy or girl named then becomes "It," and the game continues.

Variation:

Instead of girls or boys to name, children can name—

   - Old Testament or New Testament characters.

   - Something man-made or something God-made.

   - A symbol found on a musical staff or the title of a hymn or chorus.

FINGER PLAY
(KEYBOARD RECOGNITION)

TIME: 10-15 minutes

MATERIALS NEEDED:
- pencils and paper
- a copy of labeled keyboard sheet (see page 133) for each child
- keyboard

INSTRUCTIONS:

1. Supply pencil and paper for each child.

2. Ask children to trace around their right hands. Younger children may need assistance.

3. Now ask children to number the thumb and fingers of their hand picture (thumb—1, index—2, middle—3, ring—4, pinky—5).

4. Tell children that you are going to call out the number 1, 2, 3, 4, or 5. When they hear a number, they must hold up the proper finger and wiggle it. They may use their hand picture as a reference.

5. Now provide for each child a copy of the labeled keyboard sheet.

6. Call out the number of a finger and the name of a key. Children should place the designated finger on the proper key of their keyboard picture. When they have made their choices, circulate among the children to see if they are making correct identifications. You may want to choose a child with the correct answer to demonstrate on the real keyboard.

BONES AND TONES
(WARM UP/CHROMATIC SCALE/RHYTHM)

TIME: 5-10 minutes

MATERIALS NEEDED:
- song—"Dem Bones" (sung or on tape)
- sticks or rhythm instruments (optional)
- tape player (optional)

INSTRUCTIONS:

Use the traditional spiritual "Dem Bones" as a warm-up, for both bodies and vocal chords.

1. *Bodies:* Children lie flat on the floor and make their bodies limp. As they listen to the song, they "wake up" or move *just that part* that is mentioned in the song.

2. *Vocal chords:* Repeat the song, asking children to stand very still, moving only their mouths and voices, up and down the scale with the music.

3. *All together, now!* Repeat the song once more. This time cut loose—sing *and* move through the song, just for the fun and the rhythm!

VARIATION:

- Accompany this activity with sticks—or with a whole band of rhythm instruments.
- Divide your choir into three groups: singers, players, and movers. Then do the activity three times, rotating groups so all children have an opportunity to do each part.

WHEN THE MUSIC STOPS
(MUSIC SYMBOLS/GENERAL REVIEW OF MUSICAL OR BIBLICAL FACTS)

TIME: 10-15 minutes

MATERIALS NEEDED:
- chairs for all children
- cards or stickers bearing musical symbols
- musical instrument or recorded music

INSTRUCTIONS:

1. Set up chairs as you would for a game of musical chairs.

2. Tape musical symbols or notes under several chairs.

3. When the music stops and everyone is seated, ask children to look under their chairs. Those who find musical symbols must identify them by the proper name.

VARIATION:

- Put stickers under selected chairs. Children who end up on stickered chairs must tell one thing for which they are thankful...something they like about another classmate...an answer to a music or Bible-related question drawn from a hat.

STANDING TALL
(SIGHT READING)

TIME: 10-15 minutes

MATERIALS NEEDED: • chalkboard and chalk

INSTRUCTIONS:

1. Divide children into two teams, and direct them to stand on opposite sides of the room.

2. With musical notation, write on the board a challenging rhythm pattern.

3. Ask the first player on team A to read and clap the rhythm pattern after you set the tempo.

4. If the player does so accurately, he remains standing. If he misses, he is seated and the first player on team B tries.

5. Repeat the process until all players on both teams have had a turn; the team with the most members standing wins.

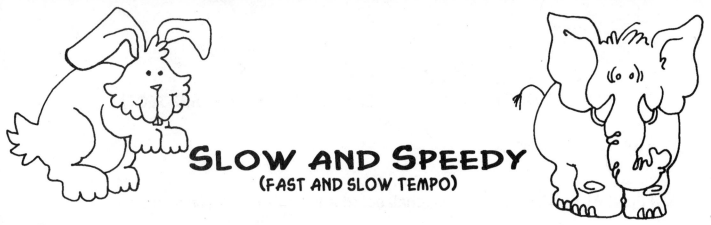

SLOW AND SPEEDY
(FAST AND SLOW TEMPO)

TIME: 5-10 minutes

MATERIALS NEEDED:
- musical instrument on which tempos may be demonstrated
  OR
- recorded examples of music in different tempos

INSTRUCTIONS:

1. Children stand in a circle.

2. Discuss and demonstrate the meaning of the word *tempo*. When the tempo is fast, the music moves swiftly like a rabbit. When the tempo is slow, the music moves slowly like an elephant.

3. Ask children to listen carefully as you play music in different tempos. When they hear a fast tempo, they pretend to be rabbits. When they hear a slow tempo, they pretend to be elephants. (They may stand in place and make appropriate body movements, or—if space is available—they may walk around in a circle as they pretend.)

Pizza Party!
(Team Game—Reinforcement, Review for any Subject)

Time: 10-20 minutes

Materials Needed: • chalkboard and chalk (red, yellow, and white)

Instructions:

1. Use white chalk to draw a large circle on the board. Divide this "pizza" up into any even amount of pieces.

2. Divide class into two teams: Cheese (yellow) and Pepperoni (red)

3. Prepare a list of music or Bible-related questions on the lesson you want to review.

4. When a member of the cheese team answers correctly, she may color one piece of the pizza to look like cheese. When a member of the pepperoni team answers correctly, he may claim a piece of the pizza by adding pepperoni. If a question is *not* answered correctly, the turn simply goes to the opposite team.

5. Continue the game until the entire pizza is colored in. The team with the most pieces of pizza wins.

Variation:

- Add more teams by adding more ingredients: green peppers, brown mushrooms, etc.
- Rename the game "Piece of Cake" and use different colors of "icing" to identify pieces.
- Surprise children with a real pizza or cake party when the game is over!

Ten Quick Questions
(Review—Any Subject)

Time: 10-15 minutes

Materials Needed:
- a treble staff floor mat (just one), and 1 moveable whole note for each team
  OR
- staff drawn on board and chalk

Instructions:

1. Use your permanent treble staff floor mat or a hand-drawn staff on the chalkboard to chart progress or keep score for "Ten Quick Questions." Mark off ten narrow measures on the staff, and provide a construction-paper whole note (or chalk) for each team.

2. Divide class into three or four teams. Draw a circle on the floor in front of each team. Ask each team to place a whole note in the first measure on the staff.

3. Be ready to ask ten to twenty Bible or music-related questions. To prepare for each question, one member of each team stands beside his designated circle. Whatever players think they know the answer to your question step quickly into their circles. The first person to step into a team circle gets an opportunity to answer the question aloud. If she answers correctly, she may move her team's whole note to the next measure on the staff. If she misses, the second team gets a chance. The team whose whole note reaches the double bar first wins.

It's in the Bag
(Naming Lines and Spaces)

Time: 5-15 minutes

Materials Needed:
- 1 or more bean bags
- masking tape or music staff floor mat
- open floor space

Instructions:

1. Use a prepared music staff floor mat, or create one with masking tape (it may be a treble, bass, or grand staff).

2. Lay an additional strip of tape about three feet from the staff to mark a line on which players will stand.

3. Allow children to stand on the line and take turns tossing the bean bag onto the staff.

4. Reward a point or a small prize (such as M & M's) to each child who can correctly identify the name of the line or space on which his bag lands.

Variation:
- Divide class into teams.

MAJOR/MINOR QUIZ
(DISTINGUISHING BETWEEN MAJOR AND MINOR CHORDS)

TIME: 10 minutes

MATERIALS NEEDED: • keyboard

INSTRUCTIONS:

1. Demonstrate simple major and minor chords on a keyboard, asking children to listen for the difference. (Major chords have a pleasant, happy sound; minor chords have a rather sad sound.)

2. Show them what makes the difference between the two chords by playing a C major triad, then moving the third down a half step. Let them each experiment by playing the two kinds of chords on the keyboard.

3. Explain that you will make statements that are either true or false. When they hear a *true* statement, they should respond by playing a *major* chord. When they hear a *false* statement, they should play a *minor* chord.

4. Call on one child at a time to respond. Use musical or Bible-related statements such as these:
   • Jesus was a Jew.
   • This is a quarter note. (Hold up picture of a note.)
   • In the Bible, Moses comes before Adam.
   • An eighth note gets more beats than a quarter note.
   Use statements that reinforce or review what you are presently teaching.

VARIATION:
   • Tempos may be demonstrated by individual children, one at a time.

SILLY SYMPHONY
(FOLLOWING THE CONDUCTOR)

TIME: 10-15 minutes

MATERIALS NEEDED:
- tape of any appropriate song
- tape player

INSTRUCTIONS:

1. Divide players into four orchestra sections: violins, clarinets, trumpets, and drums.

2. Let each section develop and practice making an appropriate sound for its section—tooting, humming, buzzing, nasal humming, etc.—and mime motions used to play their particular instruments.

3. Play the tape of a song you are learning. As the song plays, ask the players to watch the conductor to see which instruments should be playing.

4. When the conductor pantomimes the playing of an instrument, that section of the "orchestra" plays, moving in rhythm with the music.

5. When the conductor waves hands, all sections play together.

6. Players must watch the conductor carefully to know when to play!

VARIATION:

- Intermediate children may be allowed to take turns conducting, using correct time patterns.

DIATONICALLY OPPOSED
(DIATONIC SCALE—A RELAY GAME)

TIME: 10-15 minutes

MATERIALS NEEDED: • chalkboard and chalk

INSTRUCTIONS:

1. Draw two staves, side by side on the chalkboard. Locate middle C on each staff.

2. Divide the class into two relay teams.

3. Explain that members of each team are to take turns, relay fashion, writing the notes of the C major scale in sequence on the staff without missing a line or space. Each player writes one note, then passes the chalk to the next player on his team.

4. The first player on each team begins at the D above middle C and each subsequent player adds to the sequence, stepwise up the staff to top line F and then back down to middle C.

5. The first team to finish the pattern correctly wins. If a line or space is omitted, the team is disqualified.

VARIATION:

• Use the same procedure to create a chromatic scale.

KEY SCAN
(KEYBOARD/SHARPS AND FLATS)

TIME: 10-15 minutes

MATERIALS NEEDED:
- a copy of labeled keyboard sheet (see page 133) for each child
- pencils
- keyboard floor mat, or real keyboard that all can see

INSTRUCTIONS:

1. Supply a pencil and a copy of the keyboard page for each child.

2. Use the keyboard floor mat or a real keyboard to demonstrate how a sharp or flat symbol affects a note.

3. Then list ten random sharp or flat note names on the chalkboard. For example:
$$A^\# \ C^b \ G^\# \ D^\# \ B^b$$

4. Ask children to identify and label on their keyboard page each note you've listed.

5. Check answers by allowing children to take turns walking each answer on the keyboard floor mat, or by playing the proper note on a real keyboard.

HOW NOTE-ABLE R U?
(NAMING NOTES)

TIME: 10 minutes

MATERIALS NEEDED:
- reproducible page (below), pencils
- reproduce for each child only the part of this page that appears below the dotted line

---

HOW NOTE-ABLE R U?

Directions: Using only the names of the notes on the scale, see how many words you can create.

Now try to write a sentence or phrase using only the names of the notes on the scale.

Can you sing each word you wrote?

(20-45 MINUTES)

BACK TO THE DRAWING BOARD
(MEMORIZING SONGS, HYMNS)

TIME: 30-40 minutes

MATERIALS NEEDED:
- markers or crayons for each child
- paper

INSTRUCTIONS:

1. Divide the words of the song to be memorized into sections. Try to have at least as many sections as you have children in the class.

2. Write each section of words boldly across the top of a sheet of blank paper, one section per sheet.

3. Starting at the beginning of the song, discuss with the children the meaning of each phrase.

4. Then ask each child to choose a page he or she would like to illustrate.

5. After all words have been read and discussed (and artistic suggestions have been offered to those who wish them), provide markers or crayons and ask children to begin drawing. Encourage them to be neat, to use vivid color, and to give careful thought to the meaning of the words they are illustrating.

6. When all pages are finished and laid out in order, you will have a pictorial representation (or rebus) of the song lyrics. Hang or tape the pictures on the board or wall, and sing the song. Point to the pictures as the class sings. (If space is a problem, hold the pictures up, one by one, as the class sings.)

7. Keep the pictures for the following week so they may be used to review the song.

PRAISE RATTLES
(RHYTHM)

TIME: 20-25 minutes

MATERIALS NEEDED:

- two 8-inch to 10-inch paper plates per child
- dry beans, rice, or cereal
- crayons or markers
- stapler
- tongue depressors (optional)

INSTRUCTIONS:

1. Allow children to decorate the bottom side of both plates by drawing something that God made—or anything for which they praise him.

2. Along the edge of one side of the plate (or on the tongue depressor), the children should write their names.

3. Begin stapling the plates together at the edges and insert a handful of beans, rice, or cereal.

4. Continue to staple edges, inserting and securing tongue depressor as a handle.

5. Use these "praise rattles" as rhythm instruments to accompany a rousing group of praise songs and choruses.

TOE-RE-MI CHORUS
(SINGING FOR FUN)

TIME: 20 minutes

MATERIALS NEEDED: • fine-tip marking pens

INSTRUCTIONS:

1. Give children felt marking pens and demonstrate how to draw tiny faces on the "pillow" side of each of their bare toes.

2. Seat children in a circle with bare feet stretched out in front of them so all toes can be seen. Divide them into two or three groups, and give each group a name: Piggly Wigglies, for example, or Silly-Willies or Itsy-Bitsies.

3. Sing a familiar, fun song in which each group or chorus of toes has a definite and separate part (that is, a different phrase or line).

4. As each group of children sings their designated part, they wiggle their toes. When any one group sings, the others remain still and silent.

HOP A WHOLE STEP, HALF STEP
(IDENTIFYING WHOLE STEPS, HALF STEPS)

TIME: 15-20 minutes

MATERIALS NEEDED:
- keyboard floor mat
  OR
- any keyboard large enough to be observed by entire class

INSTRUCTIONS:

1. Spread on the floor a large-size representation of a keyboard—at least one octave.

2. Demonstrate the game by standing on a key, then "hopping" a whole step. Define and discuss a whole step.

3. Demonstrate and define a half step in the same manner.

4. Continue with several more examples until most students seem to understand.

5. Then ask students to take turns hopping either a whole step or half step, following your instructions. For example:
   > *"Stand on F. Hop a half step up. On what note are you now standing?"*
   The game can be made as simple or complex as needed for the abilities of the players.

VARIATION:
- A review version of this activity makes a good five-minute filler.

MUSICAL PANTOMIME
(INDEPENDENT DRAMA ACTIVITY)

TIME: 45 minutes

MATERIALS NEEDED:
- variety of biblical costumes and props
- variety of recorded songs and choruses (or live music!)
- cassette tape player(s)
- video equipment and tape (optional)

INSTRUCTIONS:

1. Divide class into groups of four or five children.

2. Ask each group to choose a familiar event or story from the Bible, then to plan a pantomime of the story that includes all members of the group.

3. Children must also choose an appropriate piece of music as background for their pantomime and prepare to present their story, in sequence, to the class.

4. Leave ample time for presentations.

READ ME A STORY!
(IDENTIFYING AND INTERPRETING MUSICAL DYNAMICS, TEMPOS)

TIME: 15-20 minutes

MATERIALS NEEDED:
- an easy-to-read Bible story book
- felt-tip pen
- 13 large index cards, each bearing one of the following words or symbols: piano, ritardando, forte, accelerando, rubato, crescendo, decrescendo, marcato, staccato, legato, accent, sfz

INSTRUCTIONS:

1. Ask the first player to choose a card from the pile and show it to the class.

2. The teacher then chooses a phrase or paragraph from a Bible story book; the player must read the passage in the manner indicated by the card she has drawn.

3. The class acts as a jury to decide whether the reader has correctly interpreted the musical dynamics. Thumbs up indicates a positive response; thumbs down, negative. In case of a negative response, the teacher should discuss the pre-scribed dynamic and give the reader a second chance.

4. The player returns his card to the bottom of the deck and chooses the next player.

5. The game continues as long as time and interest allow.

VARIATION:
- Using a Scripture verse or story, place dynamic markings over the words and have children take turns reading aloud the marked version. An overhead projector allows the entire class to participate in the process.

HYMN-KNOWLEDGY
(IDENTIFYING MUSICAL SYMBOLS)

TIME: 15-25 minutes

MATERIALS NEEDED: • 1 hymnal per child

INSTRUCTIONS:

1. Provide a hymnal for each child.

2. Call out one musical term or symbol that is found in the hymnal. Examples: F major key signature, sixteenth note, descant, slur, quarter rest, bass clef sign, time signature that tells you there are 3 beats to a measure.

3. As soon as a child has located in his hymnal an example of the term or symbol named, that child stands.

4. The first child who stands gets to call out the page number on which he has found the example, and all children turn to that page. The child then identifies the exact location of the example by indicating the score, measure number, beat number, etc.

5. Ask all children to locate and place a finger on the answer.

6. Continue the game as long as interest lasts or time allows.

VARIATION:

- Ask intermediate children to read silently the lyrics of each hymn located and to be ready to summarize the meaning in their own words.

FINGER SINGERS
(DIATONIC SCALE)

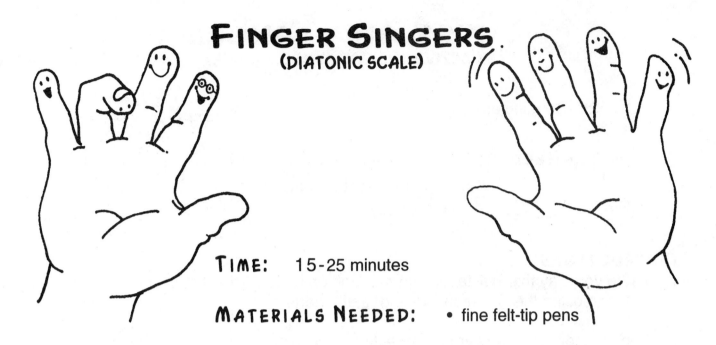

TIME: 15-25 minutes

MATERIALS NEEDED: • fine felt-tip pens

INSTRUCTIONS:

1. Ask children to draw tiny faces on the pillows of their eight fingers (not their thumbs).

2. Explain that their eight fingers now represent the eight notes of the tonic scale. (Note names or numbers may be drawn on the nail side of each finger if desired.)

3. Choose simple melodies that can be sung using only the eight notes, and let the fingers do the singing. Instruct children to move (or "nod") only the finger that is singing.

4. Children may sing along as if they were working with puppets, or they may simply move fingers to the accompaniment.

VARIATION:

• Children may label each "singer" from left to right with the sol-fa scale and sing in sol-fa syllables.

TWIST AND TANGLE
(AN ACTIVE MUSICAL-SYMBOLS GAME)

TIME: 20-30 minutes

MATERIALS NEEDED:
- 2 vinyl floor mats
- permanent black marker
- 3 x 5 cards

INSTRUCTIONS:

1. Before you play this Twister-like game, read on page 73 the instructions for creating and using the "Twist and Tangle" game parts.

2. Prepare floor mats and cards as directed in the instructions.

3. Place the two mats on the floor, and assign one mat to each team.

4. Leader chooses the top card and calls out the symbol and instructions.

5. The first player on each team finds the symbol on his mat and places the appropriate part of his body on that square.

6. As the leader calls out each additional instruction, players locate each symbol and twist or tangle their bodies as needed in order to touch all the appropriate squares.

7. If both players remain "up" without collapsing, second players from each team are added to the tangle on the mat, then third players, etc., until one team collapses.

8. The team whose member is left "up" wins.

VARIATION:
- Younger children need a smaller mat, using fewer and easier symbols.

Instructions for creating and using "Twist and Tangle" game parts

Mats
Materials Needed:
- vinyl mats—45-60-inch vinyl window shades are perfect. Shower curtains, split in half, work great, too.
- masking or vinyl tape
- permanent marking pen

1. With the tape, make a grid of 12 to 16 squares (fewer for younger children).

2. Draw a musical symbol in each square.

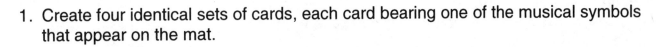

Cards
Materials Needed:
- four sets of 3 x 5 cards
- pen or marker

1. Create four identical sets of cards, each card bearing one of the musical symbols that appear on the mat.

2. Label the four card sets R.H. (right hand), L.H. (left hand), R.F. (right foot), and L.F. (left foot).

3. As each pair of players comes to the mats, call out one symbol from each set of cards. At the end of a player's turn, his hands and feet will touch four different musical symbols at the same time. When playing with younger children, you may choose to use only two sets of cards at a time.

73

HUM A NUMBER
(SINGING THE SCALE/BIBLE QUIZ)

TIME: 15-20 minutes

MATERIALS NEEDED: none

INSTRUCTIONS:

Explain to children that you will ask them Bible questions, to which the answers are numbers. When called on, they respond by *singing* the correct number of consecutive notes on the scale. Example:

Q: How many days was Jonah in the belly of the fish?

A: 1-2-3 (do-re-mi)

Other questions you can ask (create your own questions, too!):

1.   The number of persons in the Trinity (3).
2.   The number of days Lazarus was dead (4).
3.   The number of true gods (1).
4.   The number of men *thrown* into the fiery furnace (3).
5.   The number of men *seen* in the furnace later (4).
6.   The number of people in the ark (8).
7.   The number of commandments written in stone (10).
8.   The number of thieves crucified with Christ (2).
9.   The number of days of Creation (6).
10.   The number of loaves in a boy's lunch, used by Jesus (5).
11.   The number of fishermen disciples (4).
12.   The number of sisters Lazarus had (2).
13.   The number of times Naaman dipped himself in the Jordan River (7).
14.   The number of gifts brought by the Magi to the baby Jesus (3).
15.   The number of times Joshua and his people circled Jericho's wall (7).

Go Fishing!
(MUSICAL SYMBOLS)

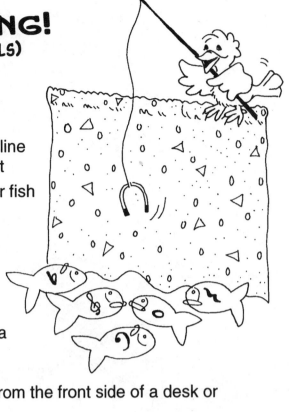

TIME: 15-20 minutes

MATERIALS NEEDED:
- "fishing pole" and line with small magnet
- construction paper fish
- paper clips
- felt-tip marker

INSTRUCTIONS:

1. Prepare fishing pole and cut 20 to 25 paper fish from construction paper. On each fish write a musical symbol. Clip a paper clip to each fish.

2. Allow children to take turns fishing in a bowl or from the front side of a desk or screen, decorated as a pond.

3. When players make a "catch," they may keep it if they can identify and define the symbol written on it. If they can't, they must throw the fish back.

4. The player with the most fish at the end of the game wins. (Collect all fish if you wish to play the game again.)

There's Music in the Air
(Craft Project/Musical Mobiles)

TIME: 30-40 minutes

MATERIALS NEEDED:

- patterns of musical symbols (see page 137)
- thin-wire coat hangers—1 per child
- wire-cutter, pliers
- tag board
- scissors, tape, glue, stapler, staples
- black or white yarn

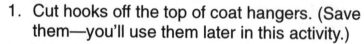

INSTRUCTIONS:

Before class...

1. Cut hooks off the top of coat hangers. (Save them—you'll use them later in this activity.)

2. Bend remainder of coat hanger into diamond shape.

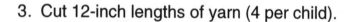

3. Cut 12-inch lengths of yarn (4 per child).

4. Cut remaining yarn into 6-, 8- and 10-inch lengths. (Distribute 6 to 8 of them per child.)

5. Copy patterns of musical symbols so they may be used for tracing, or make enough copies so children may paste them on tagboard and cut around them.

6. Gather all materials at a work table where they are easily accessible to children.

7. Assemble a sample mobile to use as a model.

During class...

1. Show model mobile to children. Relate each part to the materials on the table, and explain how it was made.

2. Ask each child to choose the following:
   - a hanger
   - a hook
   - five or six musical symbols
   - four 12-inch lengths of yarn for the top of the mobile
   - five or six shorter lengths of yarn for attaching the moving symbols

3. Children tie one 12-inch length of yarn to each corner of the hanger, then tie the loose ends of the four pieces together and attach to the hook.

4. Squeeze a drop of glue on each knot to secure.

5. Use tape to attach one end of a piece of yarn to each musical symbol.

6. Tie the opposite end of each yarn length to a corner or side of the hanger. Hang the mobile and move pieces to achieve balance. Then glue each knot to secure.

SEARCH AND COMPOSE
(COMPOSING A MELODY LINE)

TIME: 20-30 minutes

MATERIALS NEEDED:
- cut-outs of quarter notes, half notes, and whole notes (at least 10-12 notes per team)
- a large treble staff for each team (on chalkboard, floor mat, or mural paper)
- keyboard (optional)

INSTRUCTIONS:
1. Hide cut-outs of notes around the room.

2. Divide group into several teams.

3. Start a limited-time "note search," during which each team finds as many notes as possible.

4. Direct each team to a treble staff where they work cooperatively, using the notes they discovered to create a melody line of music. (They supply the time signature, bar lines, etc., and may add a note or two if those they have collected are not quite enough.

5. When all teams are ready, the teacher or a team member may try to sing or play each composed melody line.

78

LARGO

SAY IT WITH PICTURES
(ILLUSTRATING SONG LYRICS)

TIME: 45 minutes

MATERIALS NEEDED:
- white construction paper
- old magazines
- scissors, paste, crayons, markers, pencils
- a few hymnals or song books (for reference)

INSTRUCTIONS:

1. Use magazine pictures and original drawings to create a picture book to accompany a song you have learned. Examples:
   - Angels We Have Heard on High
   - For the Beauty of the Earth
   - O Beautiful for Spacious Skies
   - We Were Made to Love the Lord
   - The Six Days of Creation
   - I'm in the Lord's Army
   - Silent Night

COMPOSERS' CORNER
(WRITING/COMPOSING)

TIME: project

MATERIALS NEEDED:
- children's commercial tapes and songbooks containing familiar tunes (to use as resources)
- several Bibles and Bible storybooks
- pencil, paper

INSTRUCTIONS:

1. Ask all young composers to individually choose a Bible story or event about which they wish to compose a song lyric.

2. Then ask them to choose a song or part of a song familiar to them.

3. Their job is to "borrow" the tune and write lyrics that will fit or follow the tune as they tell the Bible story.

4. Recall several examples from the list of existing Bible story songs provided in "Bible Story Songs" (see page 118). An easy example is the use of the old camp tune, "There's a Hole in the Bottom of the Sea" as a vehicle for the new song, "There's a Road through the Bottom of the Sea," about how the children of Israel escaped miraculously from Egypt.

VARIATION:
- Writing new, original verses as additions to known hymns and choruses.

MEET AND GREET
(A PERSONALIZED INTRODUCTION OF GROUP MEMBERS)

TIME: project

MATERIALS NEEDED:
- video camera and tape
- note to parents (see instruction 3 below)

INSTRUCTIONS:

1. Video tape an introduction to each class member.
   Ask them individually to introduce themselves by—
   - Telling their name
   - Telling two things they especially like (pizza, silly jokes, etc.)
   - Telling one item of interest not generally known about them (middle name, hobby, a fear, an achievement)
   - Singing a line from a favorite song, or just naming a favorite hymn
   - Any additional item they want to share with the class

2. When all interviews have been recorded, loan the tape to the children to watch at home where they and their families can become acquainted with their class-mates. (Be sure you offer one showing of the tape at a time and place where any family who does not own a VCR may view it. Maybe your home!)

3. Use a message similar to the one below as an accompanying note to parents, in order to keep the tape circulating:

   ### *Meet the Choir!*
   This video is on loan to your young musician for one week. Please remind him or her to return it to choir next week so other members may enjoy it. Thank you!

4. At the end of the choir season, watch the tape again as a class. Children will enjoy seeing how they have changed!

ANGEL CONE CHOIR
(CRAFT PROJECT/SINGING FOR FUN)

TIME: about 45 minutes

MATERIALS NEEDED:

- yellow, white, or metallic paper
- wing and cone patterns (see page 83)
- 2-inch Styrofoam balls
- yellow/orange yarn (to simulate the angels' hair)
- glue, scissors, straight pins
- scraps of metallic trims, braids, sequins, beads, etc.
- pipe cleaners or metallic paper discs (for halos)
- short pencil stubs (optional for puppet version)

INSTRUCTIONS:

1. Following the drawings at the bottom of this page, assemble supplies to create display models of several different angels.

2. Use patterns on the next page to cut wings and cones for each child.

3. Ask children to observe models and create their own original cone angel, using the available supplies.

4. Place the completed angels in choir formation just for fun. Sing a carol, do a choral reading—or use angels as puppets for the same purpose.

VARIATION:

- Use cone angels as puppets by sticking a short pencil stub into the bottom of each Styrofoam head. A child's hand may then reach up into the cone to hold and move the angel.

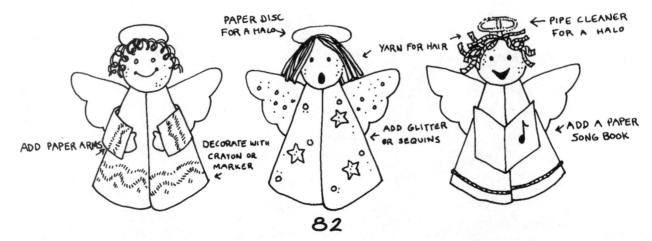

ADD PAPER ARMS

DECORATE WITH CRAYON OR MARKER

PAPER DISC FOR A HALO

YARN FOR HAIR

ADD GLITTER OR SEQUINS

PIPE CLEANER FOR A HALO

ADD A PAPER SONG BOOK

82

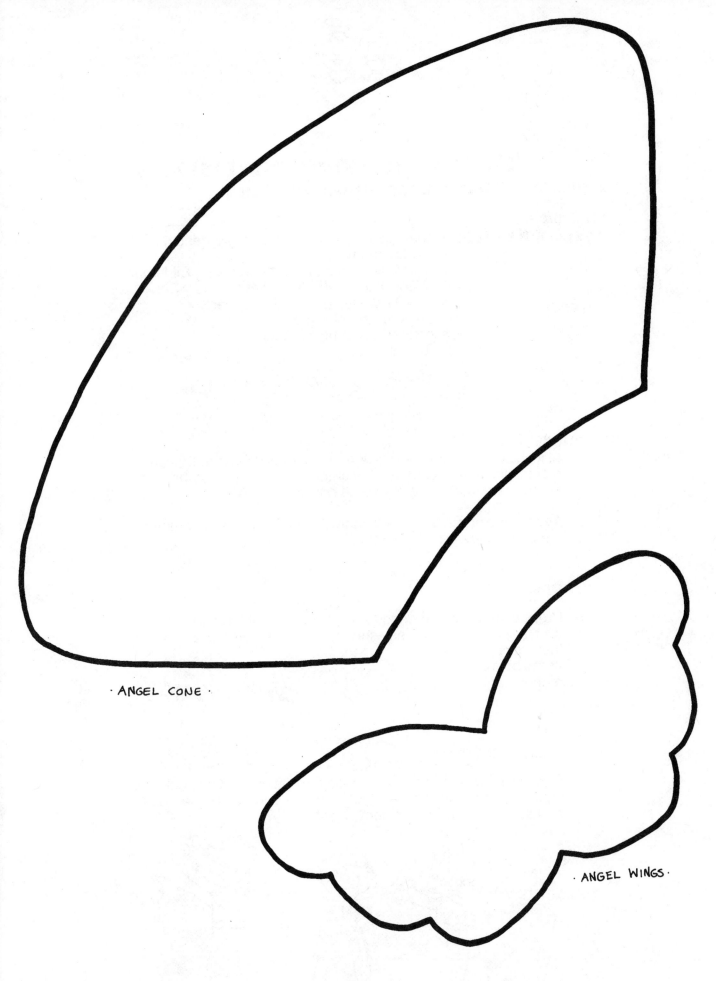

· ANGEL CONE ·

ANGEL WINGS ·

GLORY ALL AROUND US!
(ART PROJECT ILLUSTRATING A PSALM)

TIME: project

MATERIALS NEEDED:
- chart paper (or overhead transparency)
- Psalm 104 written on a chart or overhead transparency (use Living Bible paraphrase if possible), or Bibles for everyone
- 11 x 17 white construction paper
- crayons, pencils, markers
- colored construction paper for framing

INSTRUCTIONS:

1. Ask children to listen and look for words and phrases that create mental pictures of God and his creation. (Perhaps number each image instead of using the verse numbers.)

2. Assign or ask the children to individually choose one portion of the psalm they want to illustrate.

3. Provide supplies and encourage children to fill their pages with large, colorful figures—then to write the verse or phrase they have chosen at the bottom of their page.

4. Surround the classroom with these illustrations of God's glory by taping them on the walls—at least for the duration of the class, and as long thereafter as convenient.

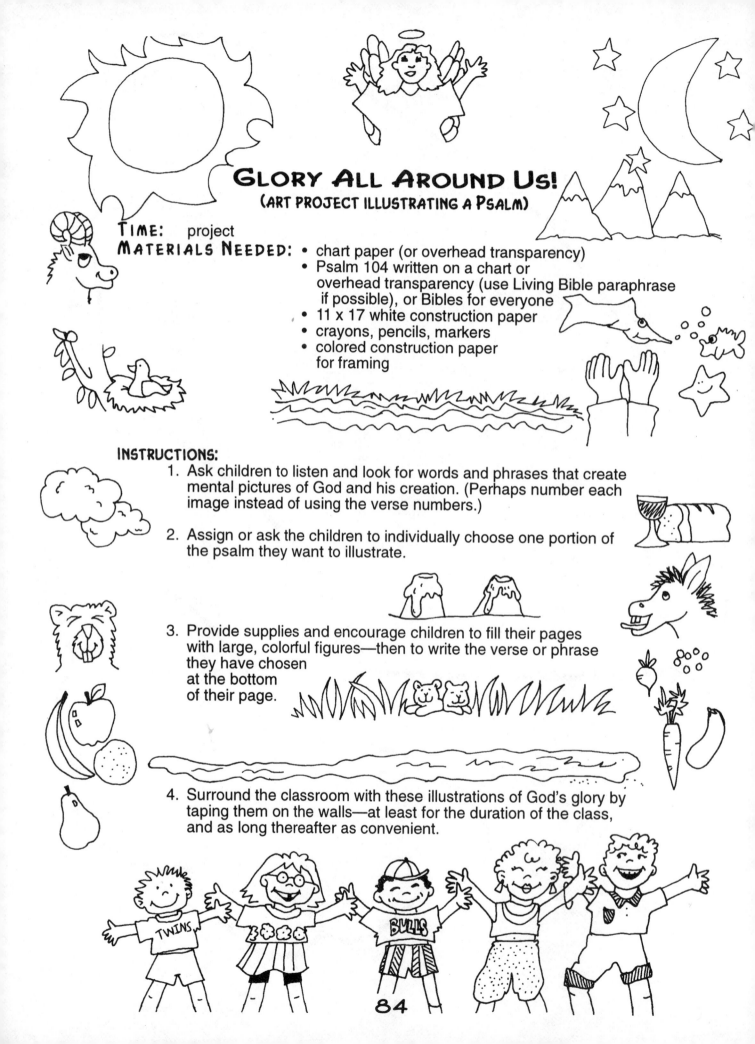

PRAISE GRAFFITI
(PRAISE EXPERIENCE)

TIME: project

MATERIALS NEEDED:

- mural paper
- markers (black and colors)
- Bibles
- Ephesians 5:19-20 written on a chart or chalkboard

INSTRUCTIONS:

1. Spread several lengths of mural paper on the floor. Use black marker to create a wall effect by drawing building blocks on the mural. (Do this ahead of time, or allow children to assist you.)

2. When the wall is ready, read aloud Ephesians 5:19-20. Discuss ways in which Christians can share a praise experience. Suggest that a "Praise Graffiti Wall" is one way of offering praise—and encouraging others to praise, as they pass by and read the wall.

3. Ask children to think of several phrases they might include on their part of the wall.

4. Assign each child a space on the mural and provide colored markers. Encourage children to be artistic as well as creative with words.

5. Display the "graffiti wall" by hanging the sections together on the wall of a hallway or classroom, or on the outside of the building.

WATER MUSIC
(EAR TRAINING/PITCH/MELODIC LINE/INTERVALS/SCALES)

TIME: project

MATERIALS NEEDED:
- 8 identical drinking glasses, bottles, or containers
- pitcher filled with water
- stainless steel spoon

INSTRUCTIONS:

1. Place empty glasses in a line on a table where everyone can see them.

2. Explain to the children that you are going to create an instrument that will play a scale. (*C D E F G A B C*, or *do re mi fa so la ti do*)

3. Gently tap the empty glasses one by one. Ask the children if they are able to hear all the different notes. (Expect them to say no, or to look puzzled.)

4. The first glass in the line (the one to your far right and the children's far left) will be *do*. Create *re* on your scale by asking a child to pour a small amount of water into the second glass. Tap gently as the child pours very slowly. Ask children to listen for *re* to emerge. (If the child overfills, simply empty some back into the pitcher.)

5. Once you have *re* established, continue by allowing another child to assist by pouring and tapping until you have *do re mi*. Use the three notes to play "Hot Cross Buns" or "Mary Had a Little Lamb." Let several children try the song.

6. Continue in the same manner, adding *fa so la ti do*. When you have a full scale, play the first phrases of "Joy to the World." Add harmony by playing "Chop Sticks."

7. If possible, let each child make his own scale. If not, let small groups of children start over and form the scale by themselves.

8. Encourage children to experiment with "water music" at home—with a parent's permission, of course.

VARIATION:

- Form two scales.
- Teach intervals.
- Label bottles *1 2 3* or *do re mi*.
- If bottles are used, you might hang them with string from a bar or rod. Paint the note/water line mark on the outside for easy refilling.
- Use food coloring to add interest.
- Have a prepared "water scale" available at all times for play and experimentation.

ABC Psalm
(WRITING A PSALM)

TIME: project

MATERIALS NEEDED:
- 8 1/2 x 11 heavy construction paper or tag
- patterns for large, 4-6-inch alphabet letters (optional)
- crayons or markers

INSTRUCTIONS:

1. Discuss the meaning of the word *psalm* (a song or hymn). Explain that many of the psalms in the Bible were written as lists—a simple format or style. Using the alphabet as a format is a good plan for thinking of ways to express praise, thanksgiving, and encouragement.

2. Distribute the cards and assign a letter of the alphabet to each child. With or without a pattern, they should use the top 6 inches of the card to create a decorative version of their alphabet letter. Then they must write a sentence or phrase that begins with that letter to add to a class "ABC Psalm."

3. Share the entire "ABC Psalm" by gathering children in sequence in a circle. Ask all the children to read their parts aloud, one at a time, in sequence.

VARIATION:

- Provide overhead transparencies on which the parts of the class psalm may be written.

All Things that have breath praise the Lord!

BE GLAD!

CAST YOUR CARES ON HIM.

SOUND INCORPORATED
(LISTENING/IMITATING SOUNDS)

TIME: project

MATERIALS NEEDED:
- cassette tape recorder and tape for each small group
- sound-effects list (for each group)

INSTRUCTIONS:

1. Divide class into small groups of three to five children.

2. Supply a tape recorder and tape for each group.

3. Distribute to each group one copy of the sound-effects list (see below).

4. Each group pretends to be a company of experts who produce sound effects for theatre or radio. The groups should meet and discuss how they might create each sound effectively, gather the tools they need, and practice their sounds. When they have perfected each sound, they should record it on their tape.

5. When all groups have had ample opportunity to complete the project, allow time for each to play their tape for the entire class to enjoy.

VARIATION:
- The task can be made more difficult by requiring that sounds be made only with musical instruments.
- Children may make their own sound-effects list to accompany a Bible story.

SOUND EFFECTS
- wind blowing through trees
- a soft, gentle rain
- a chariot race
- soldiers marching
- a storm
- a cuckoo clock ticking, then striking the hour
- popcorn popping
- cars at a race track
- waves at the seashore
- a giant sloshing through mud

Castle Choir
(PERFORMANCE STAGE SET FOR PUPPETS AND PEOPLE)

TIME: project

MATERIALS NEEDED:
- several large cardboard boxes
- drawing pens, pencils, paint, brushes
- carpet knife, scissors, tape, glue
- curtain material (optional)

INSTRUCTIONS:

1. Use large cardboard boxes or corrugated paper to construct, then draw on, a choir "castle" to use as a stage setting, from which either puppets or children may perform.

2. Create a castle-like set similar to the one pictured below, cutting many windows and doors in which performers may appear. (The openings can be considerably smaller if only puppets and not child actors use the set.)

3. When the entire group or choir sings, each member may appear in a window. Or a chorus section may be added to the side or in front of the castle, allowing the castle windows to be reserved for solos or dialogue.

4. Involve children in planning and writing a castle story—Queen Esther, for instance, or Moses or Daniel. Or the castle may be used simply as a fun, multi-use set for performance of songs, Scripture, and dialogue.

JUST MY SIZE!
(ACTION SONGS AND GAMES/DRAMA/MOVEMENT)

TIME: project

MATERIALS NEEDED:

- 2 pairs skin-colored tights (child size) for each doll
- old toddler-size clothes and shoes
- pillow stuffing
- yarn, elastic, needle and thread, button, felt scraps

INSTRUCTIONS:

1. Create two life-size, companion puppet-dolls for preschoolers. To make each doll, stuff two pairs of skin-colored tights. (Children will enjoy helping with this part, as well as with dressing them up.) Use these two stuffed tights to create the basic body: Shape one pair of tights to serve as head, neck, and arms; the second pair, as body and legs.

2. Arrange stuffing to form neck, then tie or sew at top of head. Attach body and legs as shown.

3. Dress in preschool-size clothing. (Doll should be about a head shorter than child.)

4. Use felt scraps, buttons, etc., to create face. Use yarn for hair.

5. Attach a ribbon or string to top of the puppet's head so it can be tied around the child's neck.

6. Add a piece of elastic band at each ankle and wrist so that a child can join hands and feet with the doll to operate it as a giant puppet.

7. Use puppets for action songs and games, drama, and rhythm-and-movement activities.

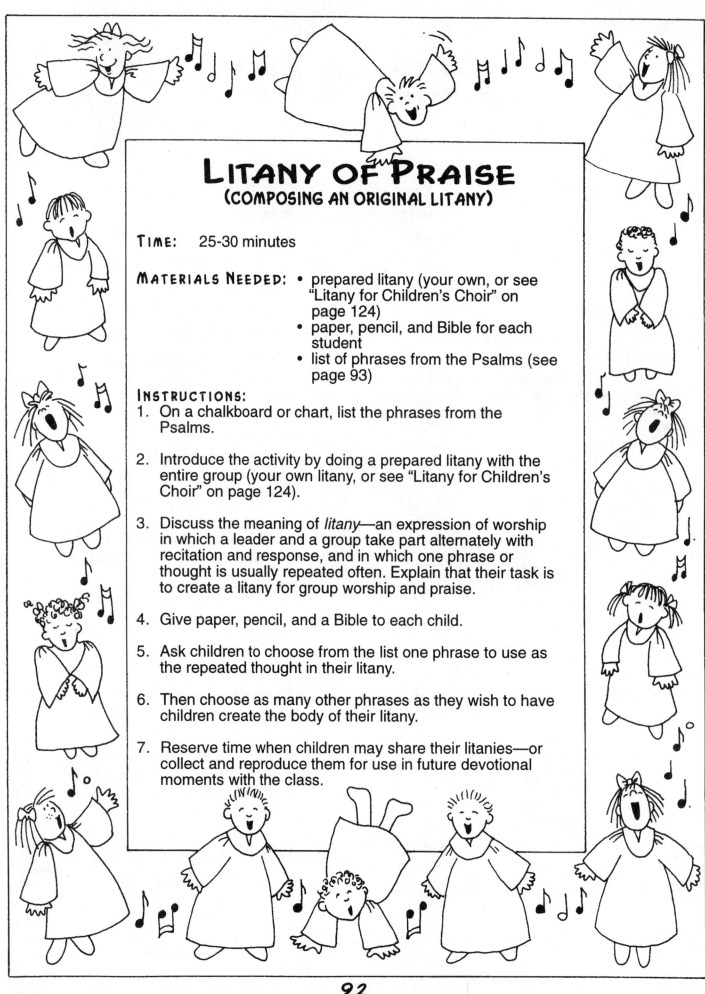

LITANY OF PRAISE
(COMPOSING AN ORIGINAL LITANY)

TIME: 25-30 minutes

MATERIALS NEEDED: • prepared litany (your own, or see
"Litany for Children's Choir" on
page 124)
• paper, pencil, and Bible for each
student
• list of phrases from the Psalms (see
page 93)

INSTRUCTIONS:

1. On a chalkboard or chart, list the phrases from the
Psalms.

2. Introduce the activity by doing a prepared litany with the
entire group (your own litany, or see "Litany for Children's
Choir" on page 124).

3. Discuss the meaning of *litany*—an expression of worship
in which a leader and a group take part alternately with
recitation and response, and in which one phrase or
thought is usually repeated often. Explain that their task is
to create a litany for group worship and praise.

4. Give paper, pencil, and a Bible to each child.

5. Ask children to choose from the list one phrase to use as
the repeated thought in their litany.

6. Then choose as many other phrases as they wish to have
children create the body of their litany.

7. Reserve time when children may share their litanies—or
collect and reproduce them for use in future devotional
moments with the class.

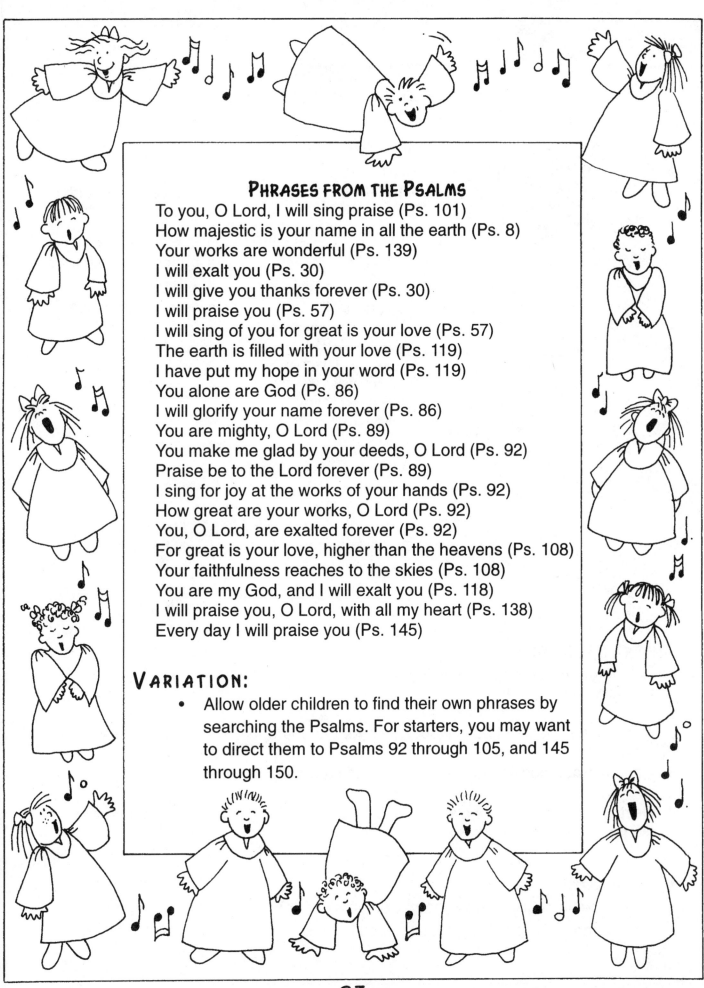

PHRASES FROM THE PSALMS

To you, O Lord, I will sing praise (Ps. 101)
How majestic is your name in all the earth (Ps. 8)
Your works are wonderful (Ps. 139)
I will exalt you (Ps. 30)
I will give you thanks forever (Ps. 30)
I will praise you (Ps. 57)
I will sing of you for great is your love (Ps. 57)
The earth is filled with your love (Ps. 119)
I have put my hope in your word (Ps. 119)
You alone are God (Ps. 86)
I will glorify your name forever (Ps. 86)
You are mighty, O Lord (Ps. 89)
You make me glad by your deeds, O Lord (Ps. 92)
Praise be to the Lord forever (Ps. 89)
I sing for joy at the works of your hands (Ps. 92)
How great are your works, O Lord (Ps. 92)
You, O Lord, are exalted forever (Ps. 92)
For great is your love, higher than the heavens (Ps. 108)
Your faithfulness reaches to the skies (Ps. 108)
You are my God, and I will exalt you (Ps. 118)
I will praise you, O Lord, with all my heart (Ps. 138)
Every day I will praise you (Ps. 145)

VARIATION:

- Allow older children to find their own phrases by searching the Psalms. For starters, you may want to direct them to Psalms 92 through 105, and 145 through 150.

Sock Singers
(Craft Project/Singing for Fun)

Time: about 45 minutes

Materials Needed:

- a collection of old socks
- pillow stuffing
- buttons, needles, thread
- markers, scissors, glue
- incidental trims

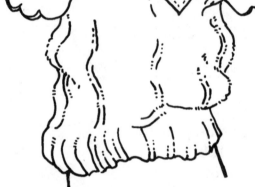

← Tuck in mouth and "catch" to bottom of "head" with needle and thread. Then stuff, leaving space for hand around mouth tuck.

Instructions:

1. Following the drawing on this page, create one or more model Sock Singer hand puppets.

2. Arrange supplies and table work space for the appropriate number of children.

3. Demonstrate models, then ask children to create their own special Sock Singers.

4. Using a table or desk as a stage, create duets, trios, quartets, and choruses of singers for fun.

Variation:

- Use as characters for dramatizing a story or song, or for making memorable announcements about future choir events.

MEDLEY

A VARIETY OF EXTRA-SPECIAL ACTIVITIES FOR CHILDREN'S CHOIR

SOL-FA SONGBIRD
(SOL-FA SCALE)

DO

TI

SOL

LA

FA

MI

RE

DO

Follow the sol-fa scale to finish Tweety Bird—then color him a happy color!

MIX AND MATCH
(MUSICAL VOCABULARY AND SYMBOLS)

Draw a line to connect each word with its matching symbol.

forte

natural

decrescendo

treble clef

mezzo piano

pianissimo

crescendo

accent

first ending

slur

sharp

bass clef

flat

VARIATION: Punch holes on the outside edges of this page, next to each word and symbol. Cut lengths of yarn, knot them, then feed them through the back of the page into each hole on the left side of the page. Ask children to connect matching words and symbols by stringing the yarn through the proper holes. This activity works especially well in a learning-center context. Laminate this page for repeated use.

UP AND DOWN THE MOUNTAIN
(SOL-FA SCALE)

do
8

___
7

___
7

___
6

___
6

___
5

___
5

___
4

___
4

___
3

___
3

___
2

___
2

do
1

do
1

See if you can climb up the musical mountain and get down again by writing the syllables up and down the scale!

OLD TESTAMENT ORCHESTRA
(ANCIENT BIBLICAL INSTRUMENTS)

Look up each Scripture reference to find the name of one or more musical instruments of praise. Then locate the instruments in the word-find puzzle.

_____   _____   _____
Psalm 137:2   Exodus 39:25   Numbers 10:2

_____   _____   _____
1 Chronicles 25:6   Daniel 3:5   1 Samuel 16:23

_____   _____
Judges 11:34   Psalm 150:3-5

ADD 'EM UP!
(NOTE VALUES)

Fill in the blanks to balance the equations.

1. $\halfnote$ + ___ = $\dottedhalf$

2. $\quarternote$ + ___ = $\halfnote$

3. $\eighthpair$ + ___ = $\wholenote$

4. $\eighthtriplet$ + ___ = $\halfnote$

5. $\halfnote$ + ___ = $\wholenote$

6. $\halfrest$ + ___ = $\dottedhalf$

7. $\quarterrest$ + ___ = $\halfrest$

8. $\eighthrest$ + ___ = $\quarterrest$

9. $\dottedhalf$ + ___ = $\wholenote$

10. $\eighthpair$ + ___ = $\dottedhalf$

11. $\quarternote$ + ___ = $\wholenote$

12. $\wholerest$ + ___ = $\wholenote$

13. $\quarternote$ + ___ = $\dottedhalf$ $\eighthtriplet$

101

JUMBLED JOY
(SIGHT READING, SEQUENCING A MELODY)

Unscramble the jumbled measures and order them so that you can read the tune "Joy to the World" from beginning to end.

Just in case you need to check your work...

BIBLE INSTRUMENT RHYMES 'N' RIDDLES
(ANCIENT BIBLICAL INSTRUMENTS/SCRIPTURE SEARCH)

**Use the Scripture references as clues to help you fill in the blanks
with the names of musical instruments found in the Bible.**

Quite like a harp
With voice a bit higher,
This stringed instrument
Is called a _____ (Psalm 92:3)

Ladies in waiting
Dance for the queen,
With rhythm played
On the _____ (Genesis 31:27)

Asaph, music man
So nimble,
Come and play
Upon your _____ (1 Chronicles 16:5)

Worshipping, praising,
And fighting battles,
They used cymbals,
Drums, and _____ (2 Samuel 6:5)

Dulcimer, psaltery,
And lyre are things
On which music is made
By plucking _____ (Psalm 33:2)

Pomegranates, spaced just right
With _____ in between
Made the priestly robes delightful
To be heard and seen. (Exodus 39:25-26)

When you hear the _____
And the _____ and the _____,
Your choice is to bow
Or end up in the fire! (Daniel 3:5-6)

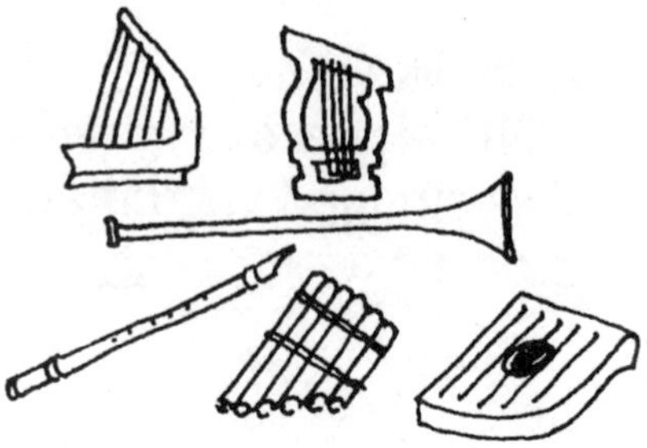

When kings were greeted
Or princes were born,
They were often heralded
By sound of the _____ (Joshua 6:4)

When your heart wants to honor
Your Lord and king,
Just lift your _____
And let it _____! (Psalm 100:1-2)

SILLY SCENARIO
(MUSIC VOCABULARY)

Use the music vocabulary on the next page and a little imagination to fill in the empty spaces so that this silly story will make sense—well, almost! (Some words are used more than once.)

Once upon a _____ there were three brothers who were _____. Their names were Allegro, Animato, and Adagio, and they were always getting into _____! They lived on _____ Lane between _____ Avenue and _____ Street, just a few blocks from a high _____ at the edge of the _____. Being _____ _____-makers, they loved to swing and hang from the rocks on the edge of the _____, just for the _____ of it!

One _____ day, at about a _____ to three, they left a _____ for their parents, hid the house _____, and _____ it to the _____ of the _____. Allegro was a master climber. He could _____ the rocks like a mountain goat. Animato was less _____ful, but even more adventuresome. He would _____ himself to a bungie _____ and leap from the craggy, _____ rocks with glee. Adagio was _____ and more cautious. He _____ed from climbing and rappelling, which were not his _____. He stayed on the _____ rocks at the _____ of the _____, _____ping chocolate pudding and _____ing in the sun.

Well, I'd like to continue this story—I _____ kept going—
but the sermon is over, the _____ has _____, and I
_____ that the church _____ is exiting the building.
Let's put this _____ of the story on _____, and I'll
give you the _____ _____ next week in
_____!

FINE!

high	eighth	sixteenth
slower	clef	grace
chord	treble	quarter
beat	tie	trill
whole	natural	refrain
note	bass	scale
triplets	C	forte
flat	sung	slur
time	score	coda
melody	staff	choir
hold	march	double time
rest	key	half

WORLD MUSIC SERIES
(SEQUENCING MUSICAL SYMBOLS AND WORDS)

What in the world is missing?
Write in the word or symbol that completes each series.

1. o o, ♩ ♩, ♩ ♩, ♪ ___, ___

2. violin, viola, cello, _____

3. $\frac{2}{4}$, $\frac{3}{4}$, ___

4. 𝄻, 𝄼, 𝄽, ___

5. d, e, f, g, ___

6. C#, D, D#, E, ___

7. o, ♩, ___, ♪

8. ♪, ♪, ♩, ___

9. ♪, ♩, ♩ ___, ___

10. tuba, trombone, _____

MUSICAL MUNCHIES
(NAMING NOTES)

Tim and Tammy are very hungry. Help them find something to eat and drink on this menu of musical munchies. Spell out the words by writing the name of each note on the line below the staff, and by using the decoder for other symbols.

THE EYES HAVE IT!
(MUSIC VOCABULARY WORD SEARCH)

Find 30 musical words in the puzzle below.
Be sure to look *up*, *down*, *backwards*, *forward*, and *diagonally*!

Z	C	L	E	F	I	N	E	T	G
P	I	A	N	O	P	O	C	O	L
R	Q	U	A	R	T	E	R	N	I
E	O	I	R	T	I	J	U	I	S
S	A	C	C	E	N	T	B	C	S
T	Q	L	R	O	H	I	A	Y	A
O	D	U	E	T	F	W	T	R	N
B	A	S	S	G	I	L	O	E	D
B	A	R	C	O	A	E	A	S	O
E	A	Y	E	K	L	T	M	T	R
A	D	N	N	O	L	O	O	U	K
T	O	V	D	X	U	A	L	T	O
W	C	H	O	R	U	S	C	O	P

ACCENT, ALTO, BAND, BAR, BASS, BEAT, CHORUS, CLEF, CODA, CRESCENDO, DUET, FINE, FLAT, FORTE, GLISSANDO, KEY, LEGATO, LOCO, PIANO, POCO, PRESTO, QUARTER, REST, RITARD, RUBATO, SLUR, SOLO, TIE, TONIC, TRIO

109

PICTURE PUZZLER
(MUSICAL SYMBOLS)

Can you find these musical symbols hidden in the picture?
Circle them. Then color the picture!

MUSIC MADNESS
(MUSICAL SYMBOLS)

Create a picture by adding your own lines to the symbol in each box.

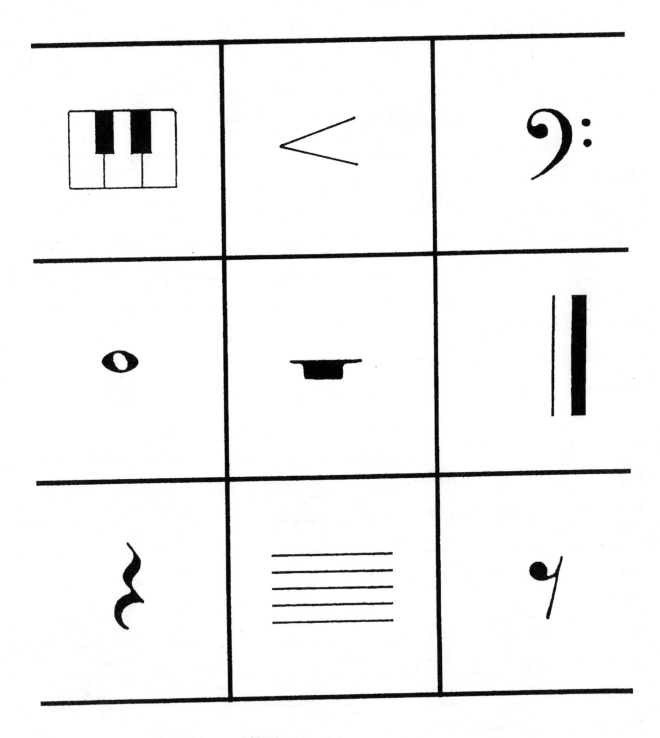

Can you tell the name of each symbol?

ALL ABOUT ME

Name_____

Age_____Grade_____Phone_____

Address_____

Birthday_____

Mom's name_____ Dad's name_____

Brothers (names and ages)_____

Sisters (names and ages)_____

One thing I like about my family_____

My favorite fun song_____

My favorite hymn or church song_____

Favorite TV program_____

Best book I ever read_____

My best friend_____

Favorite grown-up (not in my family)_____

What I like to do on a rainy day_____

Favorite sport or game_____

Hobbies_____

My favorite place to be_____

One thing that really bugs me_____

My secret dream_____

My favorite foods_____

The best trip I ever took was to_____

Something I hate to do_____

Someday I hope I get to_____

NINE NEW SONGS

RHYTHM

By Lynn Hodges

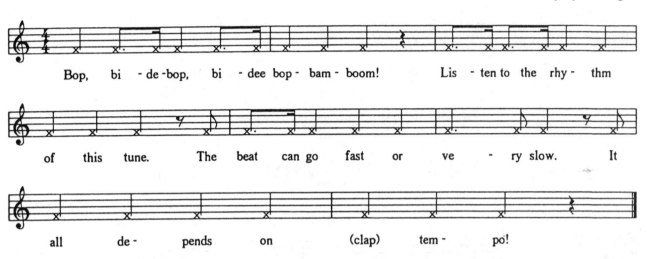

Bop, bi-de-bop, bi-dee bop-bam-boom! Lis-ten to the rhy-thm of this tune. The beat can go fast or ve-ry slow. It all de-pends on (clap) tem-po!

MARCHING TO A STEADY BEAT

By Lynn Hodges

(March tempo)

March-ing to a stead-y beat! Can-not stop to drink or eat!

FINE

Hear the rhy-thm of my feet. March-ing to a stead-y beat!

Sound off! One two! Sound off! Three four!

Left! Left! Left! Left!

LOUD - soft!

By Lynn Hodges

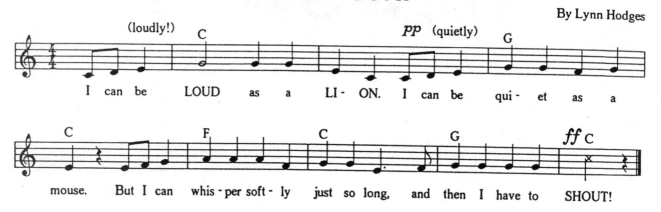

(loudly!)   C   *pp* (quietly)   G

I can be LOUD as a LI - ON. I can be qui - et as a

C   F   C   G   *ff* C

mouse. But I can whis-per soft-ly just so long, and then I have to SHOUT!

MELODY

By Lynn Hodges

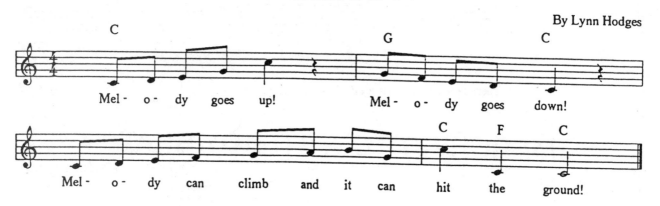

C   G   C

Mel - o - dy goes up!   Mel - o - dy goes down!

                  C   F   C

Mel - o - dy can climb and it can hit the ground!

THE MUSIC FAMILY ALPHABET

By Lynn Hodges

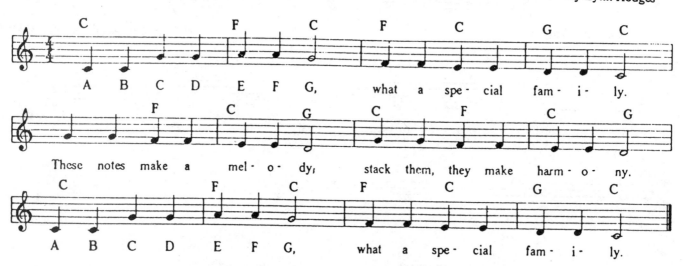

C   F   C   F   C   G   C

A B C D E F G, what a spe - cial fam - i - ly.

     F   C   G   C   F   C   G

These notes make a mel - o - dy, stack them, they make harm - o - ny.

C   F   C   F   C   G   C

A B C D E F G, what a spe - cial fam - i - ly.

S-A-T-B SONG

By Lynn Hodges

Sop - ran - o is way up high in the clouds. Al - to's a lit - tle bit low - er. The te - nor is un - der them but no - ones as low as the bass who is on the floo - R.

SO, FA, MI, SONG

By Lynn Hodges

So, fa, mi, so, fa, mi, re, so. Je - sus loves me how do I know? La, la, la, the Bi - ble says I'm His and He is mine. So, fa, mi, I'll love Him all the time!

WE ARE CHILDREN-CANON

By Lynn Hodges

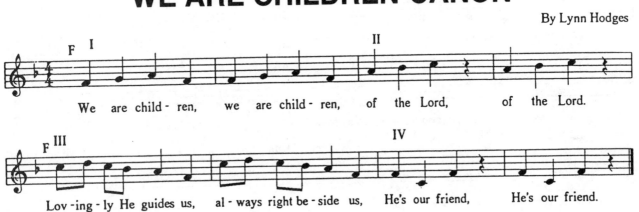

We are child - ren, we are child - ren, of the Lord, of the Lord. Lov - ing - ly He guides us, al - ways right be - side us, He's our friend, He's our friend.

ANCIENT INSTRUMENTS OF PRAISE

By Lynn Hodges and Joy MacKenzie

Lis - ten! Lis - ten! Lis - ten! Lis - ten!

Lis - ten well while you are told, names of in - stru - ments of old.

Used for wor - ship war and praise, they played songs of Bi - ble days.

Lis - ten! Lis - ten! Lis - ten! Lis - ten!

Toot -leloot -le loot toot! Toot -leloot -leloot - toot! Toot -le loot on the pipe and flute.

Toot -leloot -le loot toot! Toot -leloot -leloot - toot! Toot -le loot toot -le loot - toot -le loot.

Lis - ten! Lis - ten! Lis - ten! Lis - ten!

Boom,shake,boom,shake, boom,shake,boom,shake. It's the tam - bo - rine.

Boom,shake,boom,shake, boom,shake,boom,shake, it's a rhy - thm ma - chine.

Lis - ten! Lis - ten! Lis - ten! Lis - ten!

QUICK REFERENCE SONG LIST

Action songs
The B-I-B-L-E
The B-I-B-L-E (to the tune of B-I-N-G-O)
It's Bubbling
Clap De Hands, Stomp De Feet
Deep and Wide
Deep, Deep, Deep and the Sea
Fishers of Men
If You're Saved and You Know It
I'm in the Lord's Army
I'm Inright, Outright, Upright, Downright
    Happy All the Time
O Be Careful Little Eyes
Only a Boy Named David
This Little Light of Mine
Wide, Wide as the Ocean
The Wise Man and the Foolish Man

Praise songs
Father, I Adore You
Hallelu, Hallelu
Happiness Is the Lord
Ho Ho Ho Hosanna!
I'm a Promise!
I'm Excited in the Lord
Isn't It Grand to Be a Christian?
I've Got the Joy, Joy, Joy, Joy Down in
    My Heart
Jesus in the Morning
Jesus Loves Me
Jesus Loves Me Unconditionally
Jesus Loves the Little Children
Jesus Loves the Little Ones Like Me
Joy, Joy, My Heart Is Full of Joy
The Joy of the Lord Is My Strength
Now Unto the King Eternal, Immortal,
    Invisible
O Come Let Us Adore Him
Praise Him, Praise Him
Praise the Lord Together Singing Alleluia
Rejoice in the Lord Always

Scripture songs
Behold, Behold, I Stand at the Door
Brother James' Air (Psalm 23)
Come into His Presence
Fishers of Men
For God So Loved the World
He Is Lord
He Owns the Cattle on a Thousand Hills
How Majestic Is Thy Name
I Am the Door
I Am the Resurrection and the Life
I Will Sing of the Mercies of the Lord
    Forever
Jesus Christ Is the Way
The Lord Is My Shepherd, I'll Live for Him
    Alway
The Steadfast Love of the Lord Never
    Ceases
This Is the Day That the Lord Hath Made
This Is My Commandment That Ye Love
    One Another
Thy Word Have I Hid in My Heart
The Trees of the Field
With All My Heart

Rounds, canons, and counter melodies
Father I Adore You
Joy, Joy, My Heart Is Full of Joy
The Lord Is My Shepherd, I'll Live for Him
    Alway
Now Unto the King Eternal, Immortal,
    Invisible
Praise the Lord Together Singing Alleluia
The Shepherd Song
Song of Israel
With All My Heart

Bible-story songs
I Wonder How It Felt (to Wake Up in the
    Belly of the Whale)

Jesus Gave Her Water
Joshua Fit the Battle of Jericho
Little David Play on Your Harp
Noah (Arky, Arky)
Only a Boy Named David
Shadrach, Meshach, and Abednego
There's a Road through the Bottom of the Sea
The Six Days of Creation
The Wise Man and the Foolish Man
Zacchaeus Was a Wee Little Man

Quiet songs, prayer-time songs
All Night, All Day
All through the Night
Come into His Presence
God Is So Good
He's Got the Whole World in His Hands
Into My Heart
I've Got Peace Like a River
Kum Ba Yah
Lord Make Me Clean
O Come Let Us Adore Him
Praise the Lord Together Singing Alleluia
Thank You Lord
With All My Heart

Hymns kids should know
All Creatures of Our God and King
Amazing Grace
A Mighty Fortress
Blessed Assurance
Come Ye Thankful People, Come
Doxology

Fairest Lord Jesus
Holy, Holy, Holy
How Great Thou Art
Jesus Loves Even Me
Joyful, Joyful We Adore Thee
O How I Love Jesus
Savior Like a Shepherd Lead Us
Tell Me the Story of Jesus
To God Be the Glory
Trust and Obey
What a Friend We Have in Jesus
When I Survey the Wondrous Cross

Play songs—for marching, drumming, playing games, creating new lyrics
Alouette
Baa, Baa Black Sheep
Bill Grogan's Goat
B-I-N-G-O
Did You Ever See a Lassie?
The Farmer in the Dell
Found a Peanut
Here We Go 'Round the Mulberry Bush
Itsy Bitsy Spider
London Bridge
Mairzy Doats
Old King Cole
Old MacDonald Had a Farm
Over the River and through the Woods
Ring around the Rosy
She'll Be Comin' 'Round the Mountain
There's a Hole in the Bottom of the Sea
This Old Man

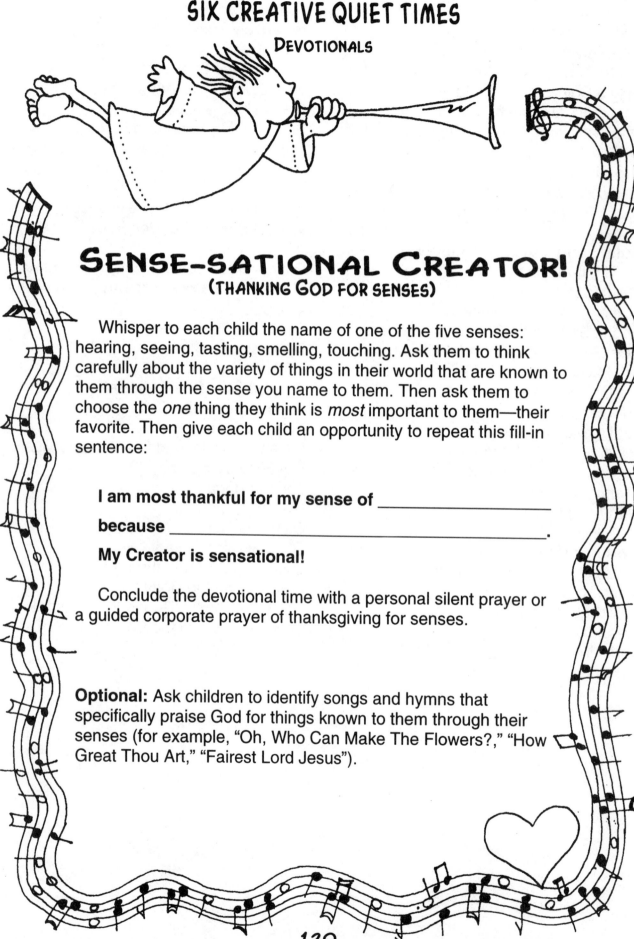

SENSE-SATIONAL CREATOR!
(THANKING GOD FOR SENSES)

Whisper to each child the name of one of the five senses: hearing, seeing, tasting, smelling, touching. Ask them to think carefully about the variety of things in their world that are known to them through the sense you name to them. Then ask them to choose the *one* thing they think is *most* important to them—their favorite. Then give each child an opportunity to repeat this fill-in sentence:

I am most thankful for my sense of _____

because _____.

My Creator is sensational!

Conclude the devotional time with a personal silent prayer or a guided corporate prayer of thanksgiving for senses.

Optional: Ask children to identify songs and hymns that specifically praise God for things known to them through their senses (for example, "Oh, Who Can Make The Flowers?," "How Great Thou Art," "Fairest Lord Jesus").

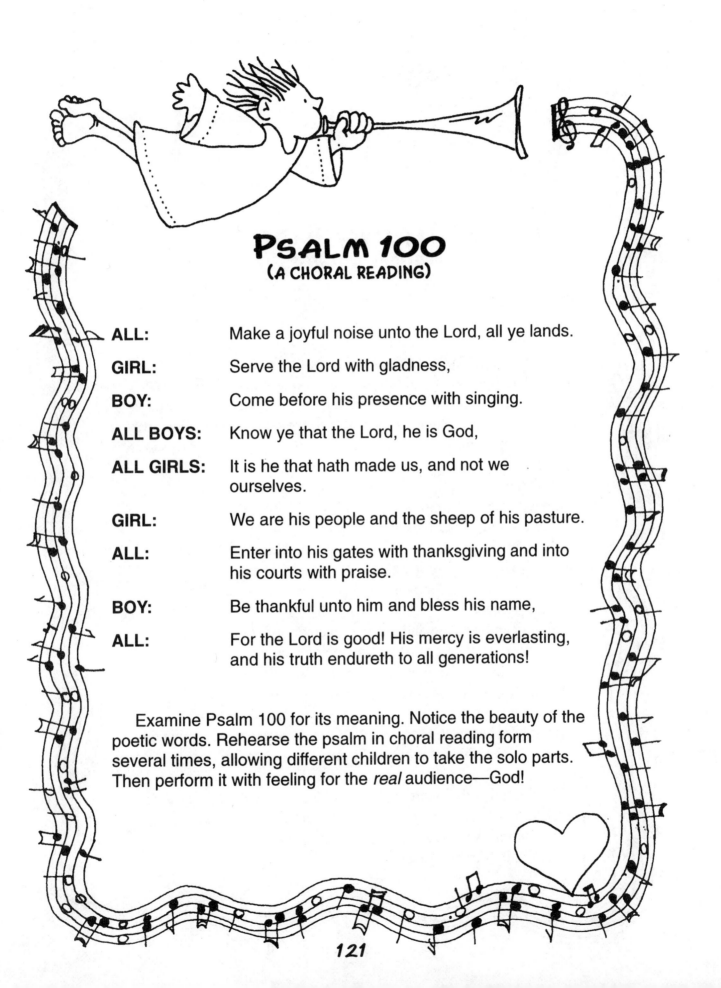

PSALM 100
(A CHORAL READING)

ALL: Make a joyful noise unto the Lord, all ye lands.

GIRL: Serve the Lord with gladness,

BOY: Come before his presence with singing.

ALL BOYS: Know ye that the Lord, he is God,

ALL GIRLS: It is he that hath made us, and not we ourselves.

GIRL: We are his people and the sheep of his pasture.

ALL: Enter into his gates with thanksgiving and into his courts with praise.

BOY: Be thankful unto him and bless his name,

ALL: For the Lord is good! His mercy is everlasting, and his truth endureth to all generations!

Examine Psalm 100 for its meaning. Notice the beauty of the poetic words. Rehearse the psalm in choral reading form several times, allowing different children to take the solo parts. Then perform it with feeling for the *real* audience—God!

WORSHIPING TOGETHER
(VERTICAL AND WORSHIP)

Ask children to join you in forming a circle. Clasp hands. Then say the following:

When we are God's children, we are all part of his family. Jesus tells us that, together we are all like one body—the body of Christ. Some people are the hands; they are the busy workers. Some are the feet; they go places. Some are the mouth; they do the speaking, etc. But there is one thing God wants us all to do together—and that is to worship him.

Sometimes when the body gets together, we talk to each other about God and how wonderful he is. We tell about the good things he does for us, and we share with one another how we feel about him. Then we sing songs like "Jesus Loves Me"..."This Little Light of Mine"..."I Have the Joy Joy Joy"..."This Is My Father's World"..."Blessed Assurance"..."Because He Lives"..."What a Friend We Have in Jesus."

Singing and praying and talking together about God are things that connect us to each other just as we are connected together in our circle. They help us love one another and help one another.

Now, still holding hands, raise them upward to the sky and be very still and quiet for just a moment. While your hands are up, look upward and whisper to God, "Hello, God. You are wonderful and I love you." *[Provide the example by doing it yourself in a stage whisper.]*

Now drop hands. When we worship God, we talk directly to him. We tell him how great he is and how important he is to us. We thank him. We give him our love. Who can think of a song that talks directly to God?

122

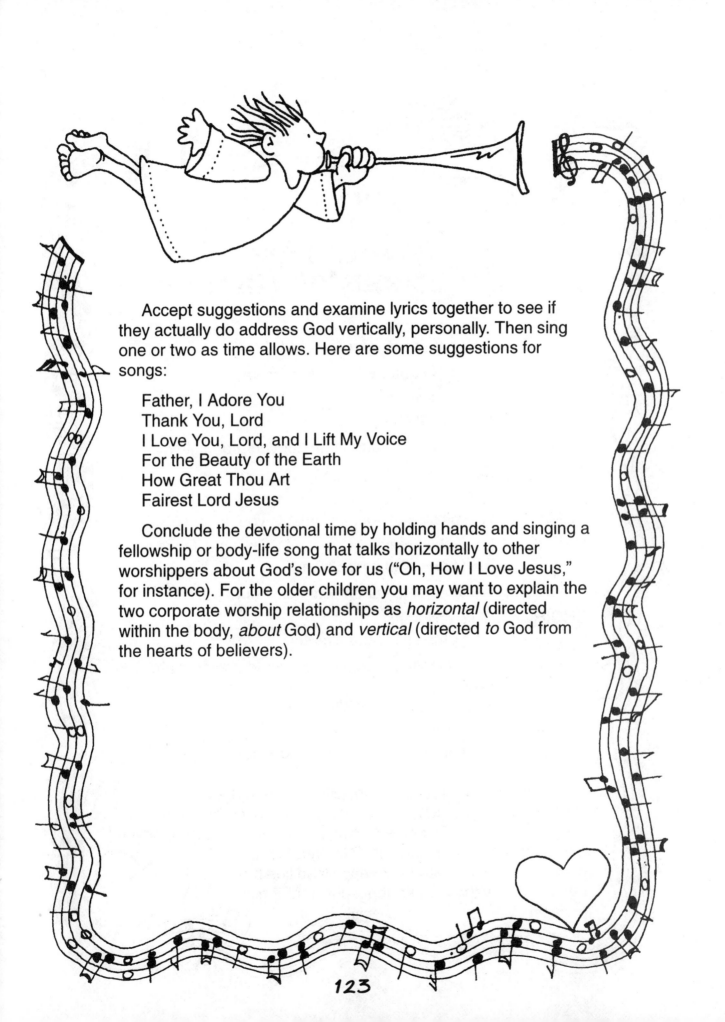

Accept suggestions and examine lyrics together to see if they actually do address God vertically, personally. Then sing one or two as time allows. Here are some suggestions for songs:

Father, I Adore You
Thank You, Lord
I Love You, Lord, and I Lift My Voice
For the Beauty of the Earth
How Great Thou Art
Fairest Lord Jesus

Conclude the devotional time by holding hands and singing a fellowship or body-life song that talks horizontally to other worshippers about God's love for us ("Oh, How I Love Jesus," for instance). For the older children you may want to explain the two corporate worship relationships as *horizontal* (directed within the body, *about* God) and *vertical* (directed *to* God from the hearts of believers).

LITANY FOR CHILDREN'S CHOIR

CHOIR: Sing, children!
          Sing praises to your God and King!

LEADER: To you, O Lord, we will sing praise.

CHOIR: Sing, children!
          Sing praises!

LEADER: We will glorify your name, for you are mighty.

CHOIR: Sing, children!
          Sing to your King.

LEADER: We will sing of you, for great is your love.

CHOIR: Sing, children!
          Sing praises to your Savior.

LEADER: We sing for joy at the work of your hand.

CHOIR: Sing, children!
          Sing praises to your Creator.

LEADER: We praise you Lord with our heart and soul and
          mind.
          You, O Lord, are exalted forever.

CHOIR: Sing, children!
          Sing praises to your God and King!

Ask children to read the litany silently. Then read
responsively, the teacher as leader, or appointing one or more
children to do so. Conclude by singing a hymn of praise, chosen
by a child or group of children. Non-readers or
preschoolers may respond to each lead line by
repeating only the words, "Sing, children! Sing
praises!"

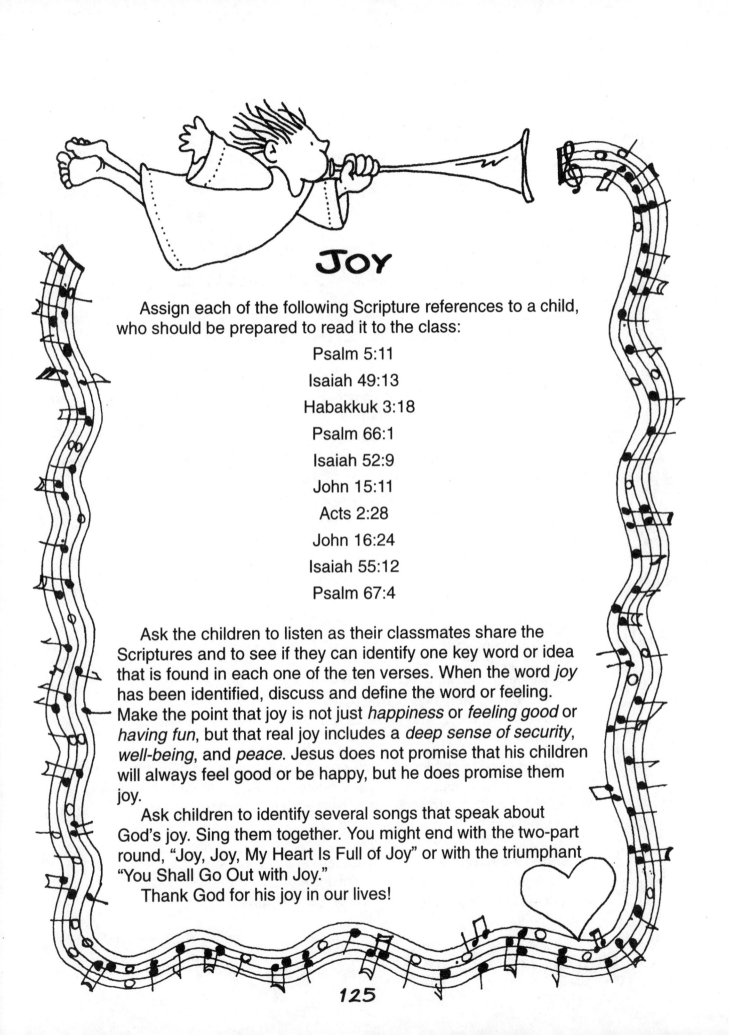

JOY

Assign each of the following Scripture references to a child, who should be prepared to read it to the class:

Psalm 5:11

Isaiah 49:13

Habakkuk 3:18

Psalm 66:1

Isaiah 52:9

John 15:11

Acts 2:28

John 16:24

Isaiah 55:12

Psalm 67:4

Ask the children to listen as their classmates share the Scriptures and to see if they can identify one key word or idea that is found in each one of the ten verses. When the word *joy* has been identified, discuss and define the word or feeling. Make the point that joy is not just *happiness* or *feeling good* or *having fun*, but that real joy includes a *deep sense of security*, *well-being*, and *peace*. Jesus does not promise that his children will always feel good or be happy, but he does promise them joy.

Ask children to identify several songs that speak about God's joy. Sing them together. You might end with the two-part round, "Joy, Joy, My Heart Is Full of Joy" or with the triumphant "You Shall Go Out with Joy."

Thank God for his joy in our lives!

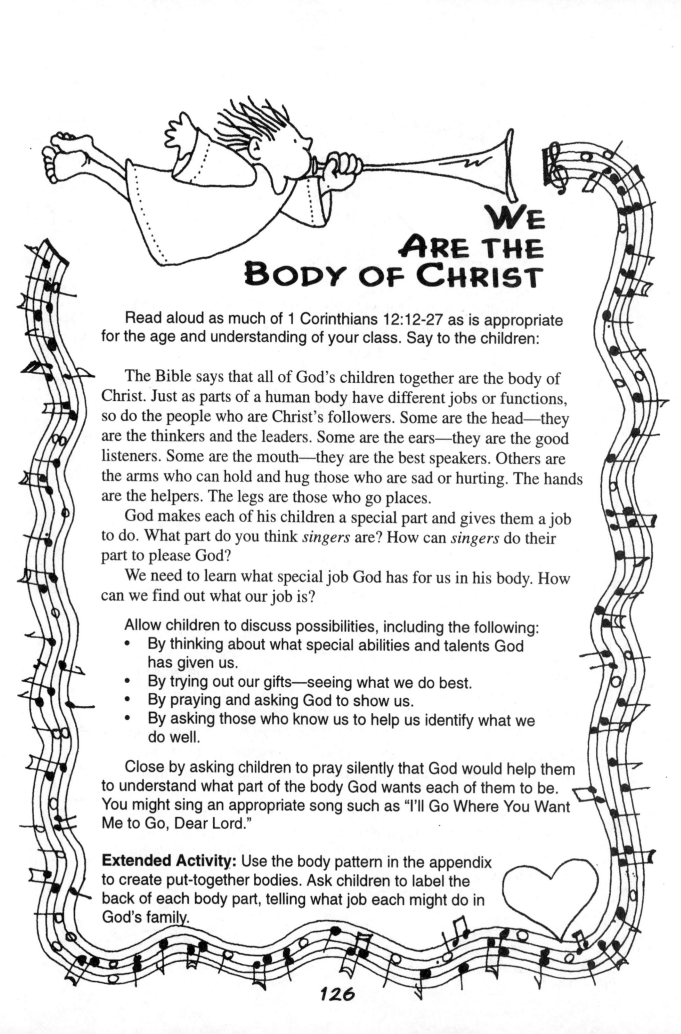

WE ARE THE BODY OF CHRIST

Read aloud as much of 1 Corinthians 12:12-27 as is appropriate for the age and understanding of your class. Say to the children:

The Bible says that all of God's children together are the body of Christ. Just as parts of a human body have different jobs or functions, so do the people who are Christ's followers. Some are the head—they are the thinkers and the leaders. Some are the ears—they are the good listeners. Some are the mouth—they are the best speakers. Others are the arms who can hold and hug those who are sad or hurting. The hands are the helpers. The legs are those who go places.

God makes each of his children a special part and gives them a job to do. What part do you think *singers* are? How can *singers* do their part to please God?

We need to learn what special job God has for us in his body. How can we find out what our job is?

Allow children to discuss possibilities, including the following:
* By thinking about what special abilities and talents God has given us.
* By trying out our gifts—seeing what we do best.
* By praying and asking God to show us.
* By asking those who know us to help us identify what we do well.

Close by asking children to pray silently that God would help them to understand what part of the body God wants each of them to be. You might sing an appropriate song such as "I'll Go Where You Want Me to Go, Dear Lord."

Extended Activity: Use the body pattern in the appendix to create put-together bodies. Ask children to label the back of each body part, telling what job each might do in God's family.

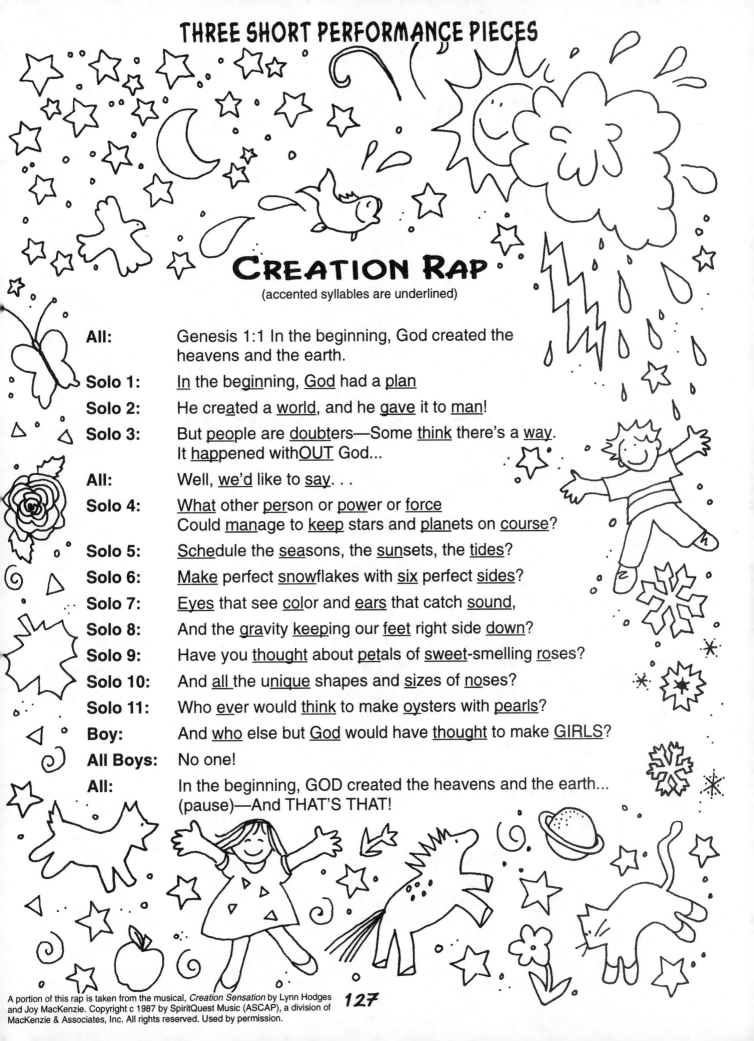

THREE SHORT PERFORMANCE PIECES

CREATION RAP

(accented syllables are underlined)

All: Genesis 1:1 In the beginning, God created the heavens and the earth.

Solo 1: In the beginning, God had a plan

Solo 2: He created a world, and he gave it to man!

Solo 3: But people are doubters—Some think there's a way. It happened withOUT God...

All: Well, we'd like to say. . .

Solo 4: What other person or power or force Could manage to keep stars and planets on course?

Solo 5: Schedule the seasons, the sunsets, the tides?

Solo 6: Make perfect snowflakes with six perfect sides?

Solo 7: Eyes that see color and ears that catch sound,

Solo 8: And the gravity keeping our feet right side down?

Solo 9: Have you thought about petals of sweet-smelling roses?

Solo 10: And all the unique shapes and sizes of noses?

Solo 11: Who ever would think to make oysters with pearls?

Boy: And who else but God would have thought to make GIRLS?

All Boys: No one!

All: In the beginning, GOD created the heavens and the earth... (pause)—And THAT'S THAT!

127

An Easter Celebration

Boys: *(with gusto)* Rejoice!

Girls: Rejoice!

All: REJOICE!

All: Hallelujah! He is risen!

Solo: What a day of gladness!

Solo: What a day to sing!

All: Sing to the Lord a new song!

Solo: Shout to the God of our salvation.

All: Christ is risen!

Solo: He is risen from the grave

Girls: *(loud whisper)* He's alive!

Boys: *(louder)* He's alive!

All: *(even louder)* He's ALIVE!

All: HALLELUJAH!

With congregation, sing "Christ the Lord Is Risen Today."

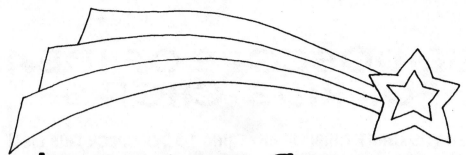

INTROIT FOR CHRISTMAS

All: A king is coming!

Solo 1:   A new ruler is going to arrive.

Solo 2:   He will bring peace to our world.

Solo 3:   He will bring light!

Solo 4:   He will be born in Bethlehem of Judea

Girls: ...In a stable!

All: He will be called Wonderful!

Solo 5:   Counselor!

Solo 6:   The MIGHTY GOD!

Solo 7:   The Everlasting Father

Boys: *(loud whisper)* The Prince of Peace!

Solo 8:   He will heal our sickness,

Solo 9:   He will bring love!

Solo 10:   He will die for us,

All: He IS love! The king HAS come!

Girl: He is HERE!

Solo 11:   All the earth shall worship him and shall sing unto him,

All: O Come, let us adore him! Christ the Lord!

Solo singing voice: O come, let us adore him

High voices: O come, let us adore him

All voices: O come, let us adore him—Christ the Lord!

Invite the congregation to join on all verses of the hymn "O Come All Ye Faithful."

KALEIDOSCOPE OF IDEAS FOR KIDS' CHOIRS

WHEN YOU CAN'T THINK OF ANYTHING TO DO, CHECK THIS LIST!

add-on songs

compose-your-own-verse songs

rounds and canons

counter melodies

vocalization

match tones

harmonizing

"building" chords

note recognition

march, clap, snap, tap

hand motions

rhythm games

rhythm bands

mimic playing instruments

play "Name That Tune"

do the "Hokey Pokey"

whistling contest

silly rhymes (some original)

jump-rope chants

tongue twisters

riddles

Simon Says

team games

experiment with high and low sounds

relays

create sound-effects stories

matching games

listening centers

treasure hunts

puzzles (hidden word, crossword)

mazes

hidden pictures

word search

Scripture memory games

write a litany

write a song

Bible sword drill

hymnal sword drill

Name that Scripture!

Scripture, rebus style

pantomime, drama

letters to Bible characters

responsive readings

video tape a song or skit

mirror (echo) singing

choral reading

musical story books

variations on Musical Chairs

GRACE NOTES

A Few Frills

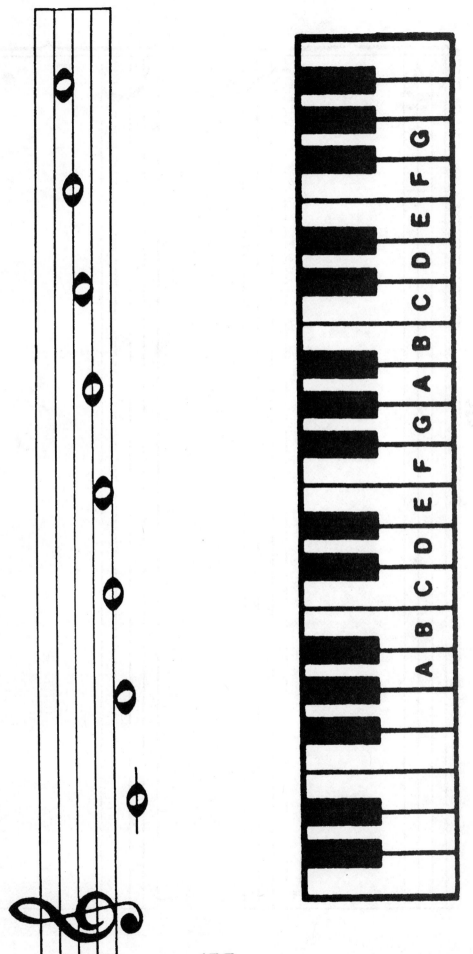

134

FLASH CARDS

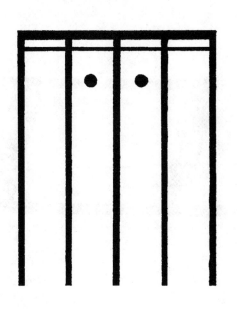

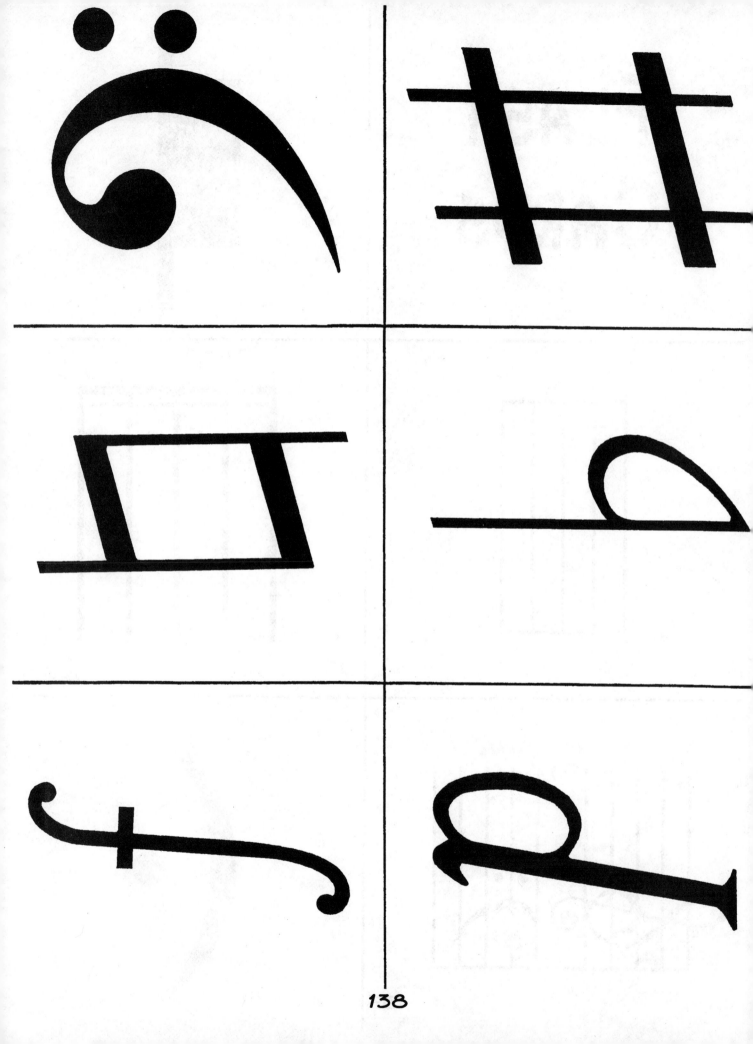

WE PRAISE HIM
(POSITIVE REINFORCEMENT/PRAISE)

Take pictures of choir members in different combinations: solos, duets, trios, quartets and chorus groups—singing and playing instruments. Then use the pictures to create a "We Praise Him" bulletin board similar to the one pictured on this page. (A preschool board might say "Wee Praise Him.")

Expand this idea if you want by forming small performance groups—trios, quartets, quintets, etc.—and allowing each to work on a special presentation. ("Welcome the Jordanaires Juniors...the Young Discovery Singers...the Cathedral Quintet!")

SETTING SAIL FOR A SENSATIONAL CHOIR SEASON
(RECRUITING)

This board adds creative flair to your recruiting process. Attach a string on a pencil to the "Passenger List." You may also include a page of nautical stickers that recruits can stick on their clothing as they sign up.

OPTIONAL: Dress up your choir staff in nautical garb during sign-up season!

Try making your own rocking boat !

MISSING PERSON
(RECRUITING)

For boy choir member, trim off lower strands of hair.

Peer pressure (and parent pressure) will add to the effectiveness of this bulletin board advertisement for choir recruits. As each member signs the roster, you may also write his/her name on one of the "person patterns" and add it to the board.

NOTE: Use a bright-colored construction paper for the question mark, so it will stand out!

ALL BY YOURS-"ELF" SCALE
(MANIPULATIVE BULLETIN BOARD IDEA—KEY SIGNATURES)

Attach to the board an envelope containing construction-paper sharps and flats that can be used to change key signatures. Give each of eight children an elf "note" and ask them to place it on the correct line or space.

This is a manipulative board that can be used by children over several class sessions to practice and review their knowledge of key signatures.

GREAT IS THE LORD
AND MOST WORTHY OF PRAISE !
Psalm 48:1

PRAISE HIM FOR:

LOVING

HOLY

MRS. ANN'S
2ND GRADE
CLASS.

GREAT IS THE LORD!
(PRAISE ART)

Give children 8-inch squares of paper and ask them to fill the page with a colorful picture or word, illustrating something for which God is to be praised. Arrange their art work attractively on the bulletin board.

THE EARLY SONGBIRDS GET THE WORMS

(ATTENDANCE, PUNCTUALITY)

Use the pattern on this page to make a bird for each choir member. Prepare a bulletin board like the one pictured here, the date of your choir rehearsal, and a worm border. Reward on-timers by writing their names on a bird and letting them place it on the board. Then give each of them a real Gummi Worm to eat!

A GRADED GUIDE TO MUSICAL KNOWLEDGE

SKILLS AND CONCEPTS THAT CAN BE MASTERED BY PRESCHOOL THROUGH GRADE 1

note	half note	treble clef	musical alphabet
beat	pitch	long/short	posture
rest	half rest	bass clef	A B C D E F G
rhythm	matching pitch	staccato	breathing
quarter note	line note	staff	introduction
tempo	tone	legato	
quarter rest	space note	bar	
melody	loud/soft	echo	

SKILLS AND CONCEPTS THAT CAN BE MASTERED BY GRADES 2 AND 3

whole note	acapella	tie	mezzo
soprano	repeat sign	piano (p)	duple meter
dotted half note	round	chord	accelerando (accel.)
alto	first ending	pianissimo (pp)	triple meter
eighth note	two-part form	major chord	ritardando (rit.)
tenor	second ending	forte (f)	2/4 time signature
ledger lines	stepwise	minor chord	4/4 time signature
bass	movement	fortissimo (ff)	3/4 time signature
measure	fermata	accompaniment	Da Capo (D.C.)
harmony	intervals (2nd,3rd,	crescendo (cresc.)	Dal Segno (D.S.)
bar line	4th)	facial expression	Coda
unison	accent	diminuendo (dim.)	Fine
double bar	dynamics	meter	

SKILLS AND CONCEPTS THAT CAN BE MASTERED BY GRADES 4-6

sixteenth note	accidental	diaphragm	triple meter (3/4)
n.b. (no breath)	simile (sim.)	descant	form (ABA, ABACA)
sixteenth rest	flat	solfege	compound meter
marcato (marc.)	pure tone	counter melody	intervals
triplet	sharp	sight singing	common time (C—4/4)
rubato (rub.)	vowel formation	modulation	(5th, 6th, 7th, octave)
triad	natural	conducting	cut time (C—2/4)
poco	staggered	score	
tonic	breathing	duple meter (2/4, 4/4)	
molto	chromatic	syncopation	

CONDUCTING PATTERNS

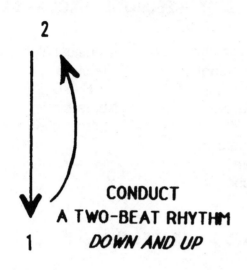

CONDUCT
A TWO-BEAT RHYTHM
DOWN AND UP

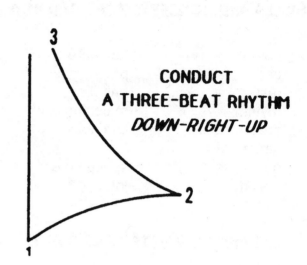

CONDUCT
A THREE-BEAT RHYTHM
DOWN-RIGHT-UP

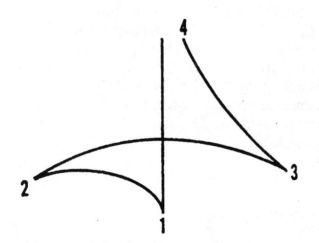

CONDUCT FOUR BEATS
DOWN-LEFT-RIGHT-UP

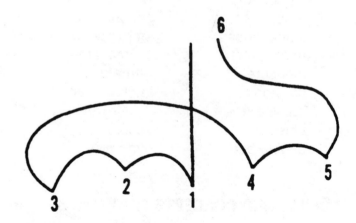

CONDUCT SIX BEATS
*DOWN-LEFT-LEFT,
RIGHT-RIGHT-UP*

BASICS IN SINGING

POSTURE

- **Sitting.** Sit with back straight, on the front of the chair, chest high, both feet on the floor, one foot slightly in front of the other.

- **Standing.** Distribute weight on both feet, knees slightly bent, chest high, head level.

- **Facial.** Keep eyebrows slightly raised, jaw completely relaxed.

BREATHING

- Keep your chest high so you can breathe low. This is called breathing from your diaphragm. (The diaphragm is a muscle which allows your lungs to expand. The area below the chest should expand and fill up with air.)

- Make no sound breathing in.

- To feel the correct way to breathe, lie on your back, flat on the floor, and breathe deeply. Feel your lungs expanding? Now stand up, remembering to keep your chest high and shoulders relaxed. Breathe. Neither your shoulders nor your chest should move.

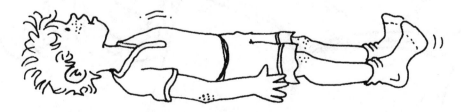

DICTION

- To enunciate (pronounce) words properly, open your mouth wide enough to get three fingers (stacked vertically) inside.

- Move your lips—a lot!

- Pronounce all consonants distinctly. This communicates to the audience how strongly you feel about what you are singing.

- Basic vowel sounds:
  a = *eh*
  e = *ih*
  i = *ah*
  o = *oh*
  u = *oo*
  Remember that a hard *r* is "nevuh" needed.

TONE

- Sing warmly with a yawny feel in the back of your throat.
- Close your mouth and feel an "inside smile." Then try the "inside smile" while you are singing.
- Always feel relaxed, never tense.
- Always warm up before singing.
- Sing an *oh* and *ah* to relax the throat.
- Never sing *loud*—sing *out*!

RESOURCES

RELIGIOUS PUBLISHERS OF CHILDREN'S MUSIC

These are most of the major U.S. publishers and suppliers of religious children's music. Write to them for catalogues and descriptions of their titles. For additional resources, visit your local Christian book store.

Benson Music Group
365 Great Circle Rd.
Nashville, TN 37228
615/742-6800

Brentwood Kids Company
316 Southgate Ct.
Brentwood, TN 37027
615/373-3950

Chorister's Guild
2834 W. Kingsley Rd.
Garland, TX 75041
214/271-1521

Genevox
127 Ninth Ave. N.
Nashville, TN 37234
615/251-2560

Integra Music
468 McNally Dr.
Nashville, TN 37211
615/831-0180

Integrity Music, Inc.
1000 Cody Rd.
Mobile, AL 36695
205/633-9000

Intrada Music Group
2222 Hill St.
Anderson, IN 46012
317/640-8211

Lillenas Publishing Company
P.O. Box 419527
Kansas City, MO 64141
816/931-1900

Maranatha Music
P.O. Box 31050
Laguna Hills, CA 92654
714/596-5778

Mel Bay Publications, Inc.
P.O. Box 66
Pacific, MO 63069
314/257-3970

Pathway Press
1080 Montgomery Ave.
Cleveland, TN 37320-7521
615/478-7614

Sparrow Distribution
101 Winners Circle
Brentwood, TN 37024-5010
615/371-6800

Spring Arbor Distributors
10885 Textile Rd.
Belleville, MI 48111
313/481-0900

Star Song Communications
2325 Crestmoor
Nashville, TN 37215
615/269-0196

Word, Inc.
5221 N. O'Conner Blvd.,
Ste. 1000
Irving, TX 75039
214/556-1900

RELIGIOUS PUBLISHERS OF CHILDREN'S BOOKS AND CURRICULA

Here are good resources for classroom activities. For additional resources, visit your local Christian book store.

Broadman Press
127 Ninth Ave. N.
Nashville, TN 37234
615/251-2560

Lion Publishing Company
1705 Hubbard Ave.
Batavia, IL 60510
708/879-0707

Shining Star Publications
P.O. Box 299
Carthage, IL 62321
217/357-3981

Concordia Publishing House
3558 South Jerrerson
St. Louis, MO 63118
314/268-1000

Moody Press
820 N. LaSalle Dr.
Chicago, IL 60610
312/329-2107

Standard Publishing
8121 Hamilton Ave.
Cincinnati, OH 45231
513/931-4050

David C. Cook Publishing Co.
850 N. Grove Ave.
Elgin, IL 60120
708/741-2400

Rhythm Band
P.O. Box 126
Fort Worth, TX 76101
817/335-2561

Warner Press, Inc.
P.O. Box 2499
Anderson, IN 46018
317/644-7721

Gospel Light Publishing
2300 Knoll Dr.
Ventura, CA 93003
805/644-9721

Scripture Press
1825 College Ave.
Wheaton, IL 60187
708/668-6000

Zondervan Publishing
5300 Patterson SE
Grand Rapids, MI 49530
616/698-6900

BOOKS

Athey, Margeret, and Gwen Hotchkiss. *A Galaxy of Games for the Music Class.* West Nyack, New York: Parker Publishing Co., Inc., 1975.

Bacak, Joyce Eilers, and Emily Crocker. *Patterns of Sound.* New Berlin, Wisconsin: Jenson Publishing, Inc., 1989.

Baker, Susan, Glennella Key, and Talmadge Butler. *Guiding Fours and Fives in Musical Experiences.* Nashville: Convention Press, 1972.

Ball, Karen, et al. *Fun Group Games for Children's Ministry.* Loveland, Colorado: Group Books, 1991.

Crisci, Elizabeth Whitney. *99 Fun Ideas for Teaching Bible Verses.* Cincinnati: The Standard Publishing Co., 1985.

Daniel, Rebecca. *Biblical Story Performances* (Christian On-Stage Series). Carthage, Illinois: Shining Star Publications, 1989.

DeVries, Betty and Mary Loeks. *Bible Activity Sheets for Special Days.* Grand Rapids: Baker Book House, 1987.

Evans, Roger. *How to Read Music.* New York: Crown Publishers, 1979.

Finley, Tom: *Incredible Stories*. Grand Rapids: Zondervan Publishing House, 1991.

Gundersen, Bev. *Memory Verse Bulletin Boards* (series). Carthage, Illinois: Shining Star Publications, 1988.

Hascall, Adelaide A. *Let's Learn Music,* books 1 and 2. Wilkinsburg, Pennsylvania: Hayes School Publishing Co., Inc., 1967.

Henderson, Larra Browning. *How to Train Singers*. West Nyack, New York: Parker Publishing Co., Inc., 1979.

Hunt, Steve, and Dave Adamson. *The Church Clip Art Book*. Grand Rapids: Zondervan Publishing House, 1988.

Ingram, Madeline D., and William C. Rice. *Vocal Techniques for Children and Youth*. New York, Nashville: Abingdon Press, 1962.

Javernick, Ellen. *Celebrate Me Made in God's Image* (and series). Carthage, Illinois: Shining Star Publications, 1988.

Klein, Joseph J., and Ole A. Schjeide. *Singing Technique*. Princeton, New Jersey: D. Van Nostrand Co., Inc., 1967.

Lynn, David. *More Attention Grabbers for 4th-6th Graders*. Grand Rapids: Zondervan Publishing House, 1990.

Lynn, David. *More Great Games for 4th-6th Graders*. Grand Rapids: Zondervan Publishing House, 1991.

Lynn, David. *More Quick and Easy Activities for 4th-6th Graders*. Grand Rapids: Zondervan Publishing House, 1991.

Lynn, David. *Quick and Easy Activities for 4th-6th Graders*. Grand Rapids: Zondervan Publishing House, 1991.

MacKenzie, Joy. *The Big Book of Bible Crafts and Projects*. Grand Rapids: Zondervan Publishing House, 1982.

MacKenzie, Joy, and Shirley Bledsoe. *The Big Book of Bible Games and Puzzles*. Grand Rapids: Zondervan Publishing House, 1982.

Nye, Robert E., and Bjornar Bergothon. *Basic Music for Classroom Teachers*. Englewood Cliffs, New Jersey: Prentice-Hall, Inc., 1962.

Nye, Robert E., and Vernice Nye. *Music in the Elementary School*. Englewood Cliffs, New Jersey: Prentice Hall, Inc., 1957.

Poelker, Kathy. *Praisin' Him*. Waco, Texas: Word Music, 1988.

Roehlkepartain, Jolene L. *Fidget Busters*. Loveland, Colorado: Group Books, 1992.

Sharon, Lois, and BramXX. *The Elephant Man*. Toronto: Lorraine Greey Publications Limited, 1989.

Spencer, Donald. *Music Reading poco a poco*. 9015 Admont Ct., Louisville, Kentucky: Donald A. Spencer, 1979.

Staton, Barbara, Merrill Staton, Marily Davidson, and Susan Snyder. *Music and You*. New York: Collier MacMillan Publishers, 1991.

Swaim, Joe and Judy. *God Made Music,* volumes 1 and 2. Taylors, South Carolina: Praise Hymn, Inc., 1984.

Wills, Maralys. *Fun Games for Great Parties*. Los Angeles: Price Stern Sloan, Inc., 1988.

SONG COLLECTIONS

Baker, Susan. *Everyday Rhythms for Children*. Nashville: Broadman Press, 1976.

Beechick, Ruth. *Teacher's Handbook of Instant Activities*. Denver: Accent Books, 1981.

Evans, Bob. *Sing-a-Long Songbook Vol. 1 and 2*. Mobile, Alabama: Integrity Music Group, 1992.

Evans, Bob. *Special Songs for Special Occasions Vol. 1 and 2*. Mobile, Alabama: Integrity Music Group, 1991.

Hill, Kathie, Janet McMahan and Joy MacKenzie. *Back At The Creekbank*. Nashville: The Benson Company, 1983.

Hodges, Lynn. *Sing-A-Long Action Songs*. Nashville: Benson Music Group, 1991.

Hopkins, Mary Rice. *Mary Rice Hopkins and Company—26 Singable Songs For The Young At Heart With Hand Motions And Actions*. Laguna Hills, California: MaranathaXX Music, 1991.

Overholtzer, Ruth. *Salvation Songs for Children*, all volumes. Warrenton, Missouri: Child Evangelism Fellowship Press, 1976.

Painter, Alice. *Activity Songs for Young Children*. Ventura, California: Gospel Light Publications, 1983.

Robertson, Clifford. *A Cappella Kids*. Laguana Hills, California: Maranatha Music's Kids' Praise Company, 1991.

Robertson, Clifford. *Famous Kids of the Bible*. Maranatha Music's Kids' Praise Company, 1991.

Sharon, Lois and Bram. *The Elephant Man*. Toronto: Lorraine Greey Publications Limited, 1989.

_____ *Sing 'n' Celebrate for Kids*. Waco, Texas: Word, Inc., 1977.

VanHook, Jim, Sarah Griffith, and Larry Mayfield. *Kids Sing Praise*, all volumes. Brentwood, Tennessee: Brentwood, Music, 1986-92.

Warren, Jean. *Piggyback Songs in Praise of Jesus*. Everett, Washington: Warren Publishing House, 1986.

POSTLUDE
Time Savers for Teachers

CLIP ART

CERTIFICATE
OF
MUSICAL MERIT

AWARDED TO _____

FOR _____

Congratulations!

_____

YOU DID IT!
GREAT
JOB!

We're Proud!

_____

 A VERY IMPORTANT NOTE...

Noteworthy:

Take 𝅘𝅥𝅮 !
(NOTE)

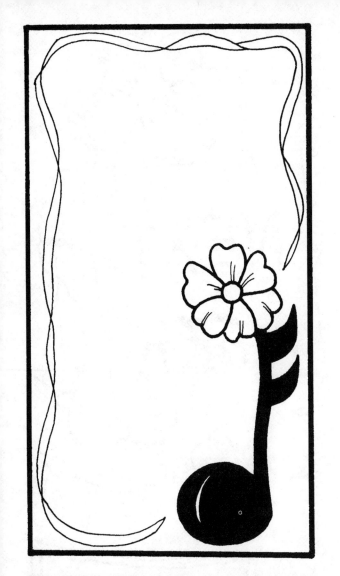

160

A BRIEF MUSIC GLOSSARY

A CAPELLA With no accompaniment.

ACCELERANDO, ACCEL. Increasing the speed.

ACCENT (>) To make one tone stronger than others.

ACCIDENTALS Music symbols placed at the left side of the head of a note that lower, raise, or return note to its normal pitch. Examples: flat (♭), natural (♮), double sharp (𝄪), double flat (♭♭).

ACCOMPANIMENT Vocal or instrumental music that supports one or more vocal or instrumental parts.

ADAGIO Slow and leisurely.

AL CODA Go to the coda.

ALLEGRO Quick, lively.

ALTO The lowest female voice; a part for this voice; instruments or voices that play or sing this part.

A TEMPO Go back to the original speed.

BARITONE A voice or instrument pitched between the bass and the tenor parts.

BAR LINE A vertical line drawn across staffs to mark off measures.

BASS The lowest voice; a part for this voice; instruments or voices which play or sing this part.

BASS CLEF (𝄢) The F clef, which locates the position of the note F on the fourth line of the staff below middle C.

BEAT A unit of time that can be counted; some beats are stronger than others.

BRASS FAMILY Instruments including French horn, trombone, trumpet, and tuba.

CANTO A song, a melody.

CAPO The beginning.

CHOIR A group of singers.

CHORD Three or more notes sounded together.

CHORUS 1) a group of singers; 2) the refrain of a song.

CHROMATIC SCALE A scale with twelve half-tones in the octave.

CLEF From the Latin word meaning *key*, a sign at the beginning of the staff that indicates the pitch of the notes on that staff.

CODA (⊕) The "tail" of a piece of music; a few bars added to the end.

COMMON TIME Time with 2, 4, 8, or 16 beats to the bar; 4/4 or C is also referred to as common time.

COMPOUND METER Meters that use triple units.

CONDUCT To direct a performance of music by means of manual and bodily motions.

COUNTER MELODY An independent melody written against another melody.

CRESCENDO, CRESC. (——————) A gradual increase in volume.

DA CAPO (D.C.) From the beginning.

DAL SEGNO (D.S.) From the sign ℅ .

DESCANT A countermelody above the melody.

DIATONIC The order of the eight tones of a major or minor scale without chromatics (that is, white keys only).

DIMINUENDO (——————) Gradually becoming softer.

DOT 1) Used after a note or rest, lengthens its value by one half; 2) used above a note to indicate staccato.

DOUBLE BAR Two vertical lines drawn through the staff, marking the end of a section, movement, or piece.

DOUBLE FLAT (♭♭) Symbol placed to the left of a note, which flattens a note's pitch two half steps.

DOUBLE SHARP (𝄪) Symbol placed to the left of a note, which raises a note's pitch two half steps.

DUET Music written for two performers or a piece of music performed by two musicians.

DYNAMICS Varying degrees of loudness or intensity.

ECHO 1) An exact repeat of a phrase; 2) a sound produced by reverberation.

EIGHTH NOTE (♪) or (♪) A unit of music notation that receives one-half the time of a quarter note.

EIGHTH REST (↯) A rest equal in value to an eighth note.

F CLEF The bass clef, which locates the position of the note F on the fourth line of the staff below middle C.

FERMATA (⌢) A hold or pause.

FINE Finish, the end.

FLAT (♭) A symbol placed before the head of a note, which lowers its pitch one-half tone.

FORM (ABA) (ABACA) The organization of a piece of music to achieve a certain logic.

FORTE (f) Loud, strong.

FORTISSIMO (ff) Very loudly.

G CLEF The treble clef, which locates the position of the note G on the second line of the staff above middle C.

GLISSANDO Sliding or gliding toward a tone.

GRACE NOTE A note of very short duration written to the left of a note and smaller.

GRANDIOSO Grandly.

GUSTO Zest.

HALF NOTE (♩) A note that receives half the value of a whole note.

HALF REST (▬) A rest the duration of a half-note.

HALF STEP Progressing up or down to the nearest note.

HARMONY 1) Musical sounds that unite and produce a pleasing sound; 2) the study of chords.

IMPROVISATION The art of creating a musical performance spontaneously.

INTERVAL The distance between two tones.

INTRODUCTION A preparatory phrase before a composition.

KEY The same as the first (tonic) note of any given scale.

LARGO A slow and broad tempo.

LEDGER LINE A short line used when needed for notes that are above or below the staff.

LEGATO Smooth.

LINE NOTE Any note that lies on a line of a staff or on a ledger line.

LOCO Used to show a return to the actual notes after an 8va transposition.

LOUD Much volume.

MAESTOSO Grandly.

MAJOR CHORDS One having a major third and perfect fifth.

MARCATO Accented, marked.

MEASURE The space or metrical unit between two bar-lines on a staff.

MELODY The tune.

METER (DUPLE, TRIPLE) The basic scheme of note values, which remains the same throughout a musical piece.

MEZZO Medium, half.

MINOR CHORD One having a minor third and perfect fifth.

MODERATO Medium tempo .

MODULATE To pass from one key to another.

MUSICAL ALPHABET The note names, A B C D E F G.

NATURAL (♮) A symbol placed before a note to cancel a preceding sharp or flat.

NOTE Symbol of musical sound, used to show the pitch and length of a musical tone.

OCTAVE An interval with eight diatonic tones; the distance between any note and the next note higher or lower that has the same name.

OSTINATO Continual, a repeated motive.

PIANISSIMO (pp) Very soft.

PIANO (p) Soft.

PICK-UP NOTE A note or notes before the first complete bar in a composition.

PITCH The highness or lowness of a tone.

POCO Little.

POLYPHONIC Music with two or more melodies.

POSTLUDE An instrumental piece played at the end of a service.

PRESTO Very fast; faster than allegro.

PSALM A sacred song or hymn.

PSALTERY A stringed instrument of the ancient Hebrews.

QUARTER NOTE (♩) A unit of music notation that receives a quarter of a whole note.

QUARTER REST (𝄽) A rest equal in time value to a quarter note.

QUARTET A composition for a group of four performers or a group of musicians performing music which has four parts.

RANGE The number of notes (highest to lowest) a voice may sing or instrument may play.

REFRAIN See CHORUS.

REPEAT A sign indicating that the music between 𝄆 and 𝄇 is to be repeated.

RHYTHM The whole feeling of movement in music; alternating tension and relaxation in the duration of the musical piece.

REST Signs that indicate a time of silence.

RITARD, RITARDANDO Delaying the tempo gradually.

ROUND Common name for a canon; each part begins the piece at a different time and repeats the piece or section at least twice.

RUBATO, RUB. An elastic, flexible tempo, accelerating and ritarding at the interpretation of the performer or conductor.

SCALE A series of notes in alphabetical order, starting with the note after which the scale is named.

SCORE A notation which shows all the parts of a musical piece arranged vertically.

SEQUE A bridge or continuance in a piece of music with no stop.

SFORZANDO (Sf, Sfz) Forced, accented.

SHARP (♯) A symbol placed before the head of a note, which raises its pitch one half tone.

SIGNATURE Signs placed at the beginning of a musical piece, indicating the key or meter.

SIXTEENTH NOTE (♪) One-sixteenth of a whole note.

SIXTEENTH REST (♦) A rest equal in value to a sixteenth note.

SLUR (⌒) A curved line drawn over or under two or more notes to indicate they are to be played or sung together.

SMOOTH Legato; with a flow.

SOLFEGE Syllables of the scale: do, re, mi, fa, so, la, ti, do.

SOLO Alone.

SOPRANO The highest voice; instruments or voices who sing or play this part.

SPACE NOTE A note that lies above or below a line on the staff.

STACCATO (·) Detached, separate; staccato notes are to be performed short and accented.

STAFF (STAVE) The horizontal five lines and four spaces on which music is written.

STRING QUARTET Chamber music for four stringed instruments; first and second violin, viola, and cello.

STRING FAMILY Instruments including violin, viola, cello, bass, and harp.

STRONG BEAT First beat after each bar line.

SYNCOPATION Any deliberate disturbance of the normal pulse of meter, accents, or rhythm.

TACET Be silent.

TEMPO The pace or speed of a musical piece.

TENOR The highest male voice; a part for this voice; instruments or voices that play or sing this part.

TIE (⌒) A bind; a curved line that appears above or below two or more notes indicating they are to be connected when sung or played.

TIME SIGNATURES Two numbers, one above the other, at the beginning of a piece which indicate the time (meter). The top number gives the number of beats in a measure; the bottom number indicates what kind of note receives one count.

TONE The quality of a sound made by an instrument or a voice.

TONIC (do) The first degree or note of a scale.

TRANSPOSING Rewriting or playing music in a different key from that in which it was originally written.

TRIAD A harmony with a root, a third, and a fifth.

TREBLE CLEF (𝄞) The G clef, which locates G on the second line of the staff above middle C.

TRIO A composition for three parts or three voices.

TRIPLE METER A grouping of time in units of three.

TRIPLET A group of three notes that fit into the time of two notes of the same value, usually indicated by a 3 and a slur.

TUTTI All; everyone is to play or sing.

TWO-PART FORM (AB) A composition that has two distinctively different sections.

UNISON Two or more voices or instruments performing the same notes or songs.

VIBRATO A slight wavering of a note.

VIVACE A quick, animated tempo.

WHOLE NOTE (o) Of the commonly used notes, the one having largest time value, receiving four beats in 4/4 meter.

WHOLE REST (▬) A rest equal in value to a whole note.

WHOLE STEP The combination of two half steps.

WHOLE TONE The interval of a major second.

WOODWIND FAMILY Instruments including bassoon, oboe, clarinet, and flute.

GOOFY GLOSSARY

ACCIDENTALS Children singing wrong notes.

ACCOMPANIMENT One who stands by the side of the performer.

BAROQUE A children's choir director after providing weekly refreshments.

BEAT A tired director, after rehearsal.

CODA The last name of the famous Italian spy, Morse.

DESCANT The opposite of *descan* (as in "Descan be sung correctly").

HARMONY A director's dream for his choir, with or without music.

LINE The stated reason a child hasn't memorized his part.

METER What every boy in the choir wants to do about the most attractive girl in the choir, but (if he's in third grade or younger) is too shy to.

REFRAIN What most directors should do more often.

REST A director's well-deserved Sunday afternoon nap.

RHYTHM An endangered phenomenon.

SHARP Dapper.

SIGHTSINGING A well-traveled musician's first love.

TIE What teachers wish they could do to an unruly student.

TRIAD The first attempt at announcing an upcoming concert.

ANSWER PAGE

NOTABLE ANSWERS
(WRITING NOTES ON A STAFF)

TIME: 10 minutes

MATERIALS NEEDED:
- the "Short Staffs" sheet (see page 135)
- pencils

INSTRUCTIONS:
1. Provide for each child a copy of the "Short Staffs" sheet on which to record answers to the following statements. Answers are written not with words, but with notes on the staff.

   - Joseph found a silver cup in Benjamin's <u>B</u> <u>A</u> <u>G</u>.

   B   A   G

   - Mary and Martha cried because Lazarus was <u>D</u> <u>E</u> <u>A</u> <u>D</u>.
   - The lame man took up his <u>B</u> <u>E</u> <u>D</u> and walked.
   - Jesus <u>F</u> <u>E</u> <u>D</u> 5,000 people with a boy's lunch.
   - Jesus taught in the temple when he was 12 years of <u>A</u> <u>G</u> <u>E</u>.
   - When Stephen was stoned, his <u>F</u> <u>A</u> <u>C</u> <u>E</u> looked like that of an angel.
   - When you want a sum, you <u>A</u> <u>D</u> <u>D</u>.
   - The devil is <u>B</u> <u>A</u> <u>D</u>.
   - The Bible says you are to honor your mom and <u>D</u> <u>A</u> <u>D</u>.

2. Encourage children to use the remaining staffs to create additional words of their own and try them out in quiz form on their friends.

36

42

HOW NOTE-ABLE R U?
(NAMING NOTES)

TIME: 10 minutes

MATERIALS NEEDED:
- reproducible page (below), pencils
- reproduce for each child only the part of this page that appears below the dotted line

- -

HOW NOTE-ABLE R U?

Directions: Using only the names of the notes on the scale, see how many words you can create.

ANSWERS WILL VARY:

ADD	BAD	CAB	BAG	FAD	ABE
BADE	FADE	FADED	CAGE	CAGED	BEE
BED	DEAD	DEB	DEAF	FED	FEED
FACE	ACE	AGE	BABE	DEED	BEAD
ADAGE	DEFACE	BAGGAGE	CABBAGE	CAFE	FEE

Now try to write a sentence or phrase using only the names of the notes on the scale.

ANSWERS WILL VARY:

A BAD DEED	DEAD ABE	FEED D BABE
BAGGAGE FEE	AGED FACE	A CABBAGE BED
C D B	BEADED BAG	FADED BAGGAGE
C DEB FACE A DEAD BEE		C D BABE-B BED

Can you sing each word you wrote?

63

STUDENT ACTIVITY SHEETS

SOL-FA SONGBIRD
(SOL-FA SCALE)

Follow the sol-fa scale to finish Tweety Bird—then color him a happy color!

97

MIX AND MATCH
(MUSICAL VOCABULARY AND SYMBOLS)

Draw a line to connect each word with its matching symbol.

forte
natural
decrescendo
treble clef
mezzo piano
pianissimo
crescendo
accent
first ending
slur
sharp
bass clef
flat

VARIATION: Punch holes on the outside edges of this page, next to each word and symbol. Cut lengths of yarn, knot them, then feed them through the back of the page into each hole on the left side of the page. Ask children to connect matching words and symbols by stringing the yarn through the proper holes. This activity works especially well in a learning-center context. Laminate this page for repeated use.

98

UP AND DOWN THE MOUNTAIN
(SOL-FA SCALE)

See if you can climb up the musical mountain and get down again by writing the syllables up and down the scale!

99

OLD TESTAMENT ORCHESTRA
(ANCIENT BIBLICAL INSTRUMENTS)

Look up each Scripture reference to find the name of one or more musical instruments of praise. Then locate the instruments in the word-find puzzle.

<u>Harp</u>
Psalm 137:2

<u>Bells</u>
Exodus 39:25

<u>Trumpets</u>
Numbers 10:2

<u>Cymbals, Lyres, Harp</u>
1 Chronicles 25:6

<u>Horn, Flute, Zither, Lyre, Harp, Pipes</u>
Daniel 3:5

<u>Harp</u>
1 Samuel 16:23

<u>Tambourine</u>
Judges 11:34

<u>Trumpet, Harp, Lyre, Tambourine, Dancing Strings, Flute, Cymbals</u>
Psalm 150:3-5

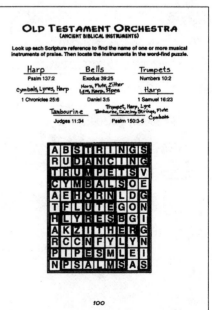

100

Add 'Em Up!
(Note Values)

Fill in the blanks to balance the equations.

1. ♩ . _♩_ = ♩ .
2. ♩ . _♩_ = ♩ .
3. ♫ . _♩_ = ♩ .
4. ♫. . _♩._ = ♩ .
5. ♩ . _♩_ = ♩ .
6. ▬ . _♩_ = ♩ .
7. ♩ . _♩_ = ♩ .
8. 𝄾 . _𝄿_ = ♩ .
10. ♫ . _♩_ = ♩ .
11. ♩ . _♩_ = ♩ .
12. ▬ . _♩_ = ♩ .
13. ♩ . _♩._ = ♩ ♫

101

Bible Instrument Rhymes 'n' Riddles
(Ancient Biblical Instruments/Scripture Search)

Use the Scripture references as clues to help you fill in the blanks with the names of musical instruments found in the Bible.

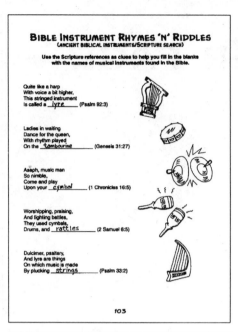

Quite like a harp
With voice a bit higher,
This stringed instrument
Is called a _lyre_ (Psalm 92:3)

Ladies in waiting
Dance for the queen,
With rhythm played
On the _tambourine_ (Genesis 31:27)

Asaph, music man
So nimble,
Come and play
Upon your _cymbal_ (1 Chronicles 16:5)

Worshipping, praising,
And fighting battles,
They used cymbals,
Drums, and _rattles_ (2 Samuel 6:5)

Dulcimer, psaltery,
And lyre are things
On which music is made
By plucking _strings_ (Psalm 33:2)

103

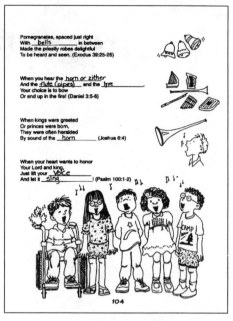

Pomegranates, spaced just right
With _bells_ in between
Made the priestly robes delightful
To be heard and seen. (Exodus 39:25-26)

When you hear the _horn_ or zither
And the _flute (pipes)_ and the _lyre_
Your choice is to bow
Or end up in the fire! (Daniel 3:5-6)

When kings were greeted
Or princes were born,
They were often heralded
By sound of the _horn_ (Joshua 6:4)

When your heart wants to honor
Your Lord and king,
Just lift your _voice_
And let it _sing_! (Psalm 100:1-2)

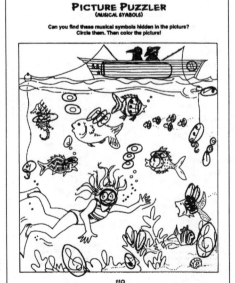

104

Silly Scenario
(Music Vocabulary)

Use the music vocabulary on the next page and a little imagination to fill in the empty spaces so that this silly story will make sense—well, almost!
(Some words are used more than once.)

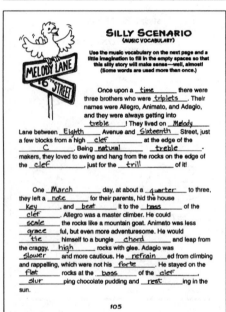

Once upon a _time_ there were three brothers who were _triplets_. Their names were Allegro, Animato, and Adagio, and they were always getting into _treble_! They lived on _Melody_ Lane between _Eighth_ Avenue and _Sixteenth_ Street, just a few blocks from a high _clef_ at the edge of the _C_. Being _natural_ _treble_-makers, they loved to swing and hang from the rocks on the edge of the _clef_, just for the _trill_ of it!

One _March_ day, at about a _quarter_ to three, they left a _note_ for their parents, hid the house _key_, and _beat_ it to the _bass_ of the _clef_. Allegro was a master climber. He could _scale_ the rocks like a mountain goat. Animato was less _grace_ful, but even more adventuresome. He would _tie_ himself to a bungie _chord_ and leap from the craggy, _high_ rocks with glee. Adagio was _slower_ and more cautious. He _refrain_ed from climbing and rappelling, which were not his _forte_. He stayed on the _flat_ rocks at the _bass_ of the _clef_, _slur_ping chocolate pudding and _rest_ing in the sun.

105

Well, I'd like to continue this story—I _coda_ kept going—but the sermon is over, the _choir_ has _sung_, and I _C_ that the church _staff_ is exiting the building. Let's put this _half_ of the story on _hold_, and I'll give you the _whole_ _score_ next week in _double time_!

FINE!

high	eighth	sixteenth
slower	clef	grace
chord	treble	quarter
beat	tie	trill
whole	natural	refrain
note	bass	scale
triplets	C	forte
flat	sung	slur
time	score	coda
melody	staff	choir
hold	march	double time
rest	key	half

106

World Music Series
(Sequencing Musical Symbols and Words)

What in the world is missing?
Write in the word or symbol that completes each series.

1. o o , ♩ ♩ , ♩ ♩ , ♪ ♪ . ♪ ♪
2. violin, viola, cello, _bass_
3. 2/4 , 3/4 , _4/4_
4. ▬ , ▬ , 𝄾 , _𝄿_
5. d , e , f , g , _a_
6. C♯, D, D♯, E, _E♯ (or F)_
7. o , ♩ , _♩_ , ♪
8. ♪ , ♩ , ♩ , o
9. ♪𝄾 , ♩𝄾 , ♩▬ , o ▬ , _o ▬_
10. tuba, trombone, _trumpet_

107

Musical Munchies
(Naming Notes)

Tim and Tammy are very hungry. Help them find something to eat and drink on this menu of musical munchies. Spell out the words by writing the name of each note on the line below the staff, and by using the decoder for other symbols.

🍎 Fruits & Veggies 🥕   ★ Protein ★
pear grape   egg   beef
pea   pepper   bread & cereal
bean cabbage   bread bran
beat date   • Beverage •
                         tea

• Decoder •

108

Look
The Eyes Have It!
(Music Vocabulary Word Search)

Find 30 musical words in the puzzle below.
Be sure to look up, down, backwards, forward, and diagonally!

```
Z C L E F L I N E T G
P I A N O P D I C O L
R Q U A R T E R N U I
E O I R D N J U I S
S A C C E N D B C S
T Q R O H I Y A
O D U E S T O W I T N
B A I S S G N O E D
B A B C O A S A S O
E A Y E R L T M I
A D N N O L O O U K
T O V D X U A T T O
W C H O R U S C O P
```

109

Picture Puzzler
(Musical Symbols)

Can you find these musical symbols hidden in the picture? Circle them. Then color the picture!

110